TOWN & COUNTY BOOKS

Staines
An illustrated record

M.M.Smithers

First published 1982

ISBN 0 7110 1125 7

Published by Ian Allan Ltd, Shepperton, Surrey;
and printed by Ian Allan Printing Ltd at their works
at Coombelands in Runnymede, England

Dedication

To Neil and Sandi with affection and
thanks for their unfailing help and
encouragement

Acknowledgements
This book owes its existence to the publishers who
had the confidence to suggest it and produce it,
and to members of the Staines Local History
Society whose painstaking research I have had the
temerity to edit and incorporate with my own work.
Particular thanks are due to S. F. Cotton, Mary
Stella Edwards, James Livermore, May
Norsworthy, the late Richard Miles, and Joy Orr.
The late Mrs Enid A. Pearse with her extensive local
knowledge and dedication to research into the local
history of Staines gave me much help and advice
for many years.

M. Maclean Smithers

Contents

Erratum, p62 note 22
In noting the originator of
information on Staines Fire Brigade,
a most unfortunate error was made
in describing R. Crimble JP as
deceased. Happily this is not the
case and author and publisher
apologise for any inconvenience or
embarrassment that might have
been caused.

Introduction

'Pry'thee, . . . let me bring thee to Staines.
(Henry V, Act II Scene 3)

So many unflattering remarks have been made about Staines by writers in the past, that it seems high time that the record should be put straight, and certainly more fairly. Staines has always been an interesting place and still is. If it is in parts unlovely to some eyes, that can equally be found in many other towns. Perhaps the most apt description is that it is a town on the road to somewhere else. It stands on the Roman road to Silchester and the west. It owes its historical importance to being on two main highways, the river and the road. Today, a third highway has been added, the air, as its boundaries take in part of London Airport. Such a position brings a state of perpetual movement in its affairs making its history more difficult to trace. Since World War 2 the population has changed rapidly both in content and size.

The earliest history of Staines has only recently begun to come to light through archaeological discovery. In 1961 at Yeoveney, on land destined for gravel extraction, a causewayed camp of some 5,000 years ago was discovered and excavated by R. Robertson-Mackay for the Ministry of Works. In 1967, during early preparation for the construction of the Moor Lane reservoir, some bones of an immature straight tusked elephant estimated to be at least 50,000 years old, were unearthed. Rebuilding in the High Street area has made it possible since 1970 to excavate and evaluate a number of sites which have yielded evidence of Roman occupation, and evidence from the 1st to the 17th centuries. Some pre-Roman evidence has also been found.[1]

Written evidence given in the Domesday Book, charters and other records show the emergence of the town from an area of intensive cultivation far in advance of its time in the 11th century to a market town of increasing importance. As a supply area for London of market garden and agricultural produce from the 14th to the mid-18th centuries, it has gradually developed into its present form of a mixed economy of retail trade, small industries, water and gravel supply, and to a decreasing extent, agriculture. It has also become, since the two world wars, an overspill area for the population of London, which has brought considerable building expansion.

Over the past 50 years many old buildings have been pulled down to make way for modern development, but for those who seek them, a number of 19th and early 20th century buildings can still be seen and even a few of earlier date.

The present stands on and exists because of the past. The past may, and indeed does have its critics. Perhaps it is as well to remember that our present will become the future's past. Will we in our turn measure up to our future critics?

Below: Thomas Sandby's bridge under construction; from a sketch by J. M. W. Turner. *J. Orr collection*

Notes on the Geography of the Staines area

From a lecture by S. F. Cotton BA

England was probably joined to the continent in the earliest times, and the Thames Valley would then have stretched from Wales to France. The 600ft layer of chalk is traceable through the Chilterns and the North Downs and then south to France. The London clay and sand to be found on Hampstead Heath on the north, and Bagshot and Cooper's Hill on the south-east, show evidence of the gravel that has been brought down from Wales. (In the northern hemisphere the pressure of a river is to the right of its valley.)

Staines is a delta area having the Colne Brook, the Wraysbury River and the River Colne feeding the main river. This is followed downstream by another delta area fed by the River Ashe, Longford River and the Eding Brook. The rich gravel deposits in the area supply an ever growing demand for the making of modern concrete buildings, roads and runways. The area around Staines is one of the flattest in the country, easy for road making, and when trade came from the west, Staines grew in importance as a crossing point over the River Thames. The very flat ground presents its own problems, in particular its liability to flooding, and the railway crossing difficulty which can only be solved by uneconomical long bridge and embankment approaches. Reservoirs too are particularly expensive to make because they cannot be built partly into a natural hill, but must have all four sides artificially built. There are, however, compensating natural advantages: supplying a long flat approach for London Airport, which is slightly offset by the local tendency to low-lying mists; also the fact that this area shares with the Fens the distinction of being the finest agricultural land in the country. There has been a big development in irrigation in the last 25 years. Small farms of 5-10 acres are most suited to the area, and the modern use of glass and its substitutes makes these small farms economically possible. The low rainfall but high humidity of the area also contributes to agricultural high productivity.

There have been developments in the conservation of the water supply. When the Queen Mary Reservoir was made, it was intended that the water drawn from the river and stored there should lie for three months before it was ready for purification and use. Modern methods have rendered this waiting period unnecessary, and under the present system river water may be purified and in use within 24 hours. Increasing demands for water in the area between Staines and London created by the increase of factories and in the population of the area demand yet more new areas of water conservation, eg the new reservoir near Moor Lane. Thus water conservation and gravel raising have given this area a very high water acreage whereby a considerable amount of agricultural land has been lost. Building programmes in their turn swallow up more of the land. The area's proximity to London makes it vulnerable to these priorities.

Below: Clarence Street c1913. Entrance to Bridge House Hotel right foreground. *Author's collection*

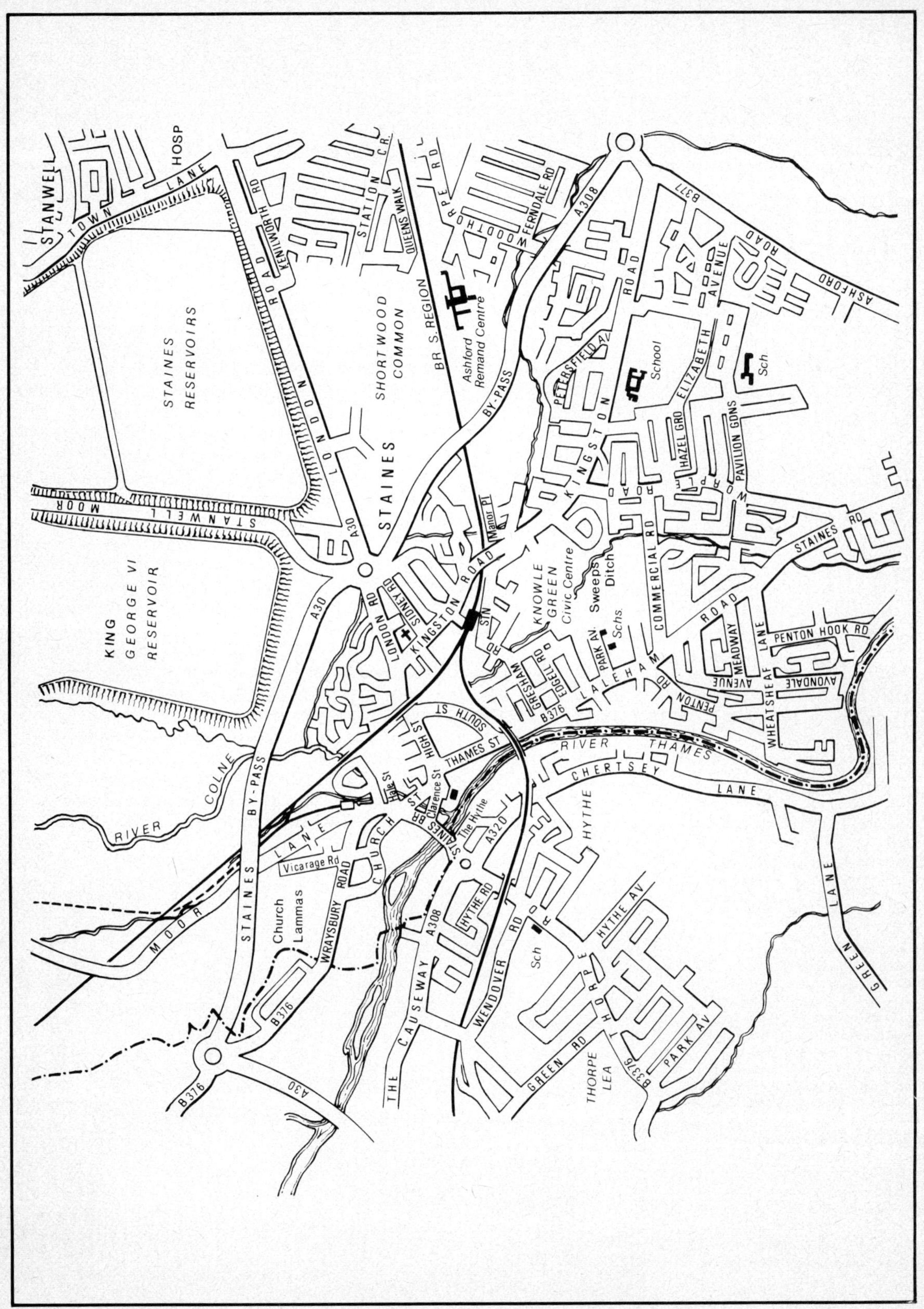

STANWELL
TOWN LANE
HOSP
STAINES RESERVOIRS
SHORT WOOD COMMON
STATION CR.
QUEENS WALK
THORPE RD
WOODTHORPE RD
FERNDALE RD
A308 ROAD
B377
ASHFORD ROAD
BR. S. REGION
Ashford Remand Centre
BY-PASS
School
PETERSFIELD AV
KINGSTON ROAD
HAZEL GRO
ELIZABETH AVENUE
THORPE RD
PAVILION GDNS
Sch
KENILWORTH RD
ROAD
LONDON
STAINES
A30
Manor Pl
KNOWLE GREEN
Civic Centre
Sweeps Ditch
COMMERCIAL RD
STAINES RD
KING GEORGE VI RESERVOIR
STANWELL MOOR
A30
LONDON RD
SUDBURY RD
KINGSTON ROAD
STN
PARK AV
Schs
ALEHAM
ROAD
PENTON RD
WHEATSHEAF LANE
AVENUE
MEADWAY
PENTON HOOK RD
AVONDALE RD
RIVER COLNE
RIVER
STAINES BY-PASS
MOOR
LANE
Vicarage Rd
Church Lammas
WRAYSBURY ROAD
CHURCH
HIGH ST
SOUTH ST
Hale St
THAMES ST
ST
Clarence St
STAINES
The Hythe
A320
GRESHAM
EDGELL RD
B376
RIVER THAMES
CHERTSEY LANE
HYTHE
HYTHE AV
GREEN LANE
B376
A30
THE CAUSEWAY
WENDOVER RD
A308
HYTHE RD
Sch
GREEN RD
THORPE LEA
PARK AV
B338

The Common Lands of Staines

The following notice is reproduced:

> **The MANOR of STAINES in the COUNTY of MIDDLESEX**
>
> # NOTICE
>
> IS HEREBY GIVEN that a COURT LEET or Law Day and a Meeting of Commoners will be holden for the said Manor on <u>Thursday, the 13th day of January 1955</u>, at 8 o'clock in the evening, at the <u>Town Hall, Staines</u>, when and where all holders of Lammas rights, all the Resiants and Freehold Tenants of the said Manor, and all Public Officers of the said Leet and Manor and others concerned in the business of such Court are required to attend.
>
> NOTE—A local custom is that a Resiant and Freehold Tenant is an Inhabitant Ratepayer of the Staines Ward.
>
> **Dated this 10th day of December, 1954.**
>
> *H. SCOTT FREEMAN,*
> Lord of the Manor, acting as his own steward.
>
> The following matters will be considered:–
> 1. Appointment of Moor Masters.
> 2.   „   „   Commoners Committee.
> 3.   „   „   Herdsman.
> 4.   „   „   Town Crier.
> 5. Any other business.
>
> Printed by J. M. STITT & Co., Ltd., ASHFORD, MIDDLESEX.

Common Rights existed long before the time of William the Conqueror. The Staines Commons today include Staines Moor, Shortwood Common, Knowle Green and Birch Green. The Commoners are those whose houses in the parish give them registered rights of 'farren' (grazing) of two cows and one horse or a lag of geese, as in the Registration of Commons Act of 1965. The grazing is managed by Moormasters who are elected at the Court Leet (an ancient manorial court) which meets at infrequent intervals as necessity arises being summoned by the Lord of the Manor.

The Lord of the Manor owns the Common Lands and the minerals beneath it, but he cannot raise the minerals if in so doing he interferes with the Commoner's rights. Hence the application to the local council for planning permission to raise gravel from Staines Moor presented a problem of some local magnitude and any attempted interference of this kind, both in the 19th century and recently, aroused a great deal of local opposition.[2] In addition, ecologists opposed extraction because the moor has been virtually undisturbed for hundreds of years and no promise by the gravel raisers to restore after extraction could therefore in a true sense restore it to what it was before. The Appeal to raise gravel from the moor was dismissed on 9 February 1981 by the Secretary of State for the Environment.

Above: The notice with which the Lord of the Manor notifies the public of a meeting of the Court Leet. *Hist Soc collection*

Right: Staines Moor is of considerable interest to historians. Aerial photographs have given evidence of Saxon cultivation and, in 1967, five incomplete bones of a straight tusked immature elephant (Mastodon?) were brought to light by an excavator during the preparations for the Metropolitan Water Board's reservoir in Moor Lane. The British Museum estimates the bones to be at least 50,000 years old. *Middlesex Chronicle*

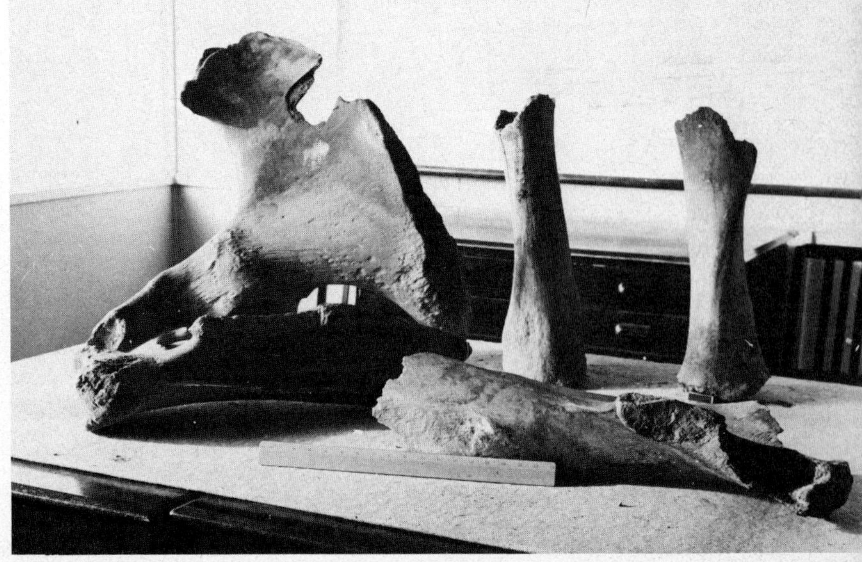

Lords of the Manor of Staines

From the 11th century the Abbot of Westminster fulfilled the function of Lord of the Manor, succeeding abbots continuing until the Reformation when the king appropriated it. It continued as a royal property until 1613. Of the worthy people who after that became Lords of the Manor perhaps the least unsung who should be better remembered is Thomas Lord Knyvett. Of an ancient and illustrious family, his forebears held royal appointments from the time of Edward I. As Sir Thomas Knyvett he was Gentleman to the Privy Chamber to Elizabeth I and an early member of the

Right: The tomb of Lord Knyvett, Stanwell Church. From 1613 the lordship of the manor could be inherited directly, sold out of the holding family (conveyed) or transferred outside the family by will. Lords of the Manor from 1613 have been: Thomas Lord Knyvett until 1622; Thomas Knyvett Esq till 1629; Sir Francis Leigh till 1638; Woolley Lee Esq until 1669; Sir William Drake till 1679; Richard Taylor, Esq and members of his family until 1890; Sir John Gibbons and members of his family till 1933; Harry Scott Freeman Esq who was steward of the manor 1901-33 and became Lord 1933-68 when his daughter Mrs D. L. Galbraith succeeded him; and finally, in 1973, the present owner Gerald Barrett, Esq, Chairman of the Greenham Sand and Ballast Co Ltd. *Author's collection*

Below: Perhaps the largest surviving monument to the importance of the moor is the access bridge known locally as the 'Cattle Bridge'. This unusual structure is actually three bridges of different dates, joined end to end: a plate girder bridge over the Great Western Railway, two yellow brick arches over the Wyrardisbury River and a single red brick span over the Southern Railway Windsor lines. *Chris Leigh*

court of James VI and I, being given on 15 August 1603 the Manor of Stanwell, which included those of West Bedfont, Hamonds or Shipcotes and Poyle. In the same year he was created Lord Knyvett. Among other honours given to him was the Lordship of the Manor of Staines in 1613. He lived at Stanwell Place and left a bequest to found a school in Stanwell named after him. Today he should surely be remembered as the man who apprehended and received the confession of Guy Fawkes. Following information concerning 'treason and plot' he was ordered in his capacity as JP of Westminster, to investigate and apprehend doubtful characters in the area of the parliament buildings. So, in a sense we owe over 300 years of 5 November bonfire nights to him! He died in 1622. His fine tomb in St Mary's Church, Stanwell, the work of the king's sculptor, Nicholas Stone, also commemorates his wife, Elizabeth, who died two months later. She had been governess to the royal children, and two of them, the princesses Mary and Sophia were in her care at Stanwell. Princess Mary died there in 1607 and her tomb in the form of a cradle is in Westminster Abbey.[3]

A more recent Lord of the Manor, the first for over 200 years to live in Staines, was Harry Scott Freeman. A son of a barrister, he became senior partner in Horne, Engall & Freeman, solicitors. He was a famous athlete in his day in several sports including hockey, sculling and sailing and was a pioneer motorist. He was also clerk of the Staines Urban District Council for many years and to the Spelthorne magistrates for 50 years. He died in October 1968. His daughter, Mrs Galbraith, succeeded him as Lady of the Manor, but after an unsuccessful appeal made jointly by her and the Greenham Sand and Ballast Co Ltd to raise gravel from Staines Moor in 1972, she sold the Lordship in 1973 to Mr Gerald Barrett, chairman of that company. In 1979 a further unsuccessful application was made by the company.

Above: Duncroft, which can be seen from Vicarage Road without entering the grounds. The estate is traceable back to 1286, but the present house was built around 1600 (it has an old rainwater head dated 1621) and considerably altered in the 18th and 19th centuries. Reputed to have been built on the site of an old hunting lodge, there are many stories about Duncroft. That King John stayed there before or after signing Magna Carta at Runnymede is not true — he slept at Windsor, a safer place for a monarch who believed his life was in danger. The story about a tunnel to Runnymede is similarly apochryphal, although, perhaps, based on a kernel of truth: there could well be a large cesspol or drain like the one at Corner Hall. *Middlesex Chronicle*

Below: The attempts by Greenhams to dig up the moor for gravel raising are not a new phenomenon and the commons have been under pressure for many years. As long ago as 1900 this cottage was erected out of funds received in compensation for the loss of certain commoners' rights. A 1980 view. *Chris Leigh*

The Military at Staines

Staines bridge has always been of strategic as well as of commercial importance, particularly as it was the only one above London Bridge until Chertsey bridge was built in 1410. Oliver Cromwell made sure that Staines bridge was under the control of his government, and his troops, both cavalry and foot soldiers, patrolled the road from Staines to London. They were garrisoned mainly at Hounslow. During the Napoleonic wars Lord Lucan, father of the Lord Lucan of Crimea fame, raised local troops, both cavalry and infantry, which were known as The Royal Spelthorne Legion. This is historically a very shadowy regiment, the exact dates of mobilisation and final stand-down do not seem to be recorded anywhere. Between about 1790 and 1798 their duty no doubt was to keep the vital roads from London to the south-west open, which meant particular attention had to be paid to the security of Staines bridge.

After the Napoleon Bonaparte scare came the Napoleon III scare when the whole country seemed to rise to the call to arms against France. General recruiting began in 1857. In 1860 a public meeting was convened by a committee of influential inhabitants of the Spelthorne Hundreds under the chairmanship of General Wood of Littleton. In a Malt House belonging to William Holgate in Staines 43 recruits were enrolled and took the oath of allegiance on 22 November 1860 before Mr R. E. Arden JP. This was the beginning of the 44th Middlesex Rifle Volunteer Corps. Originally, Staines was to be joined by men from Feltham and Sunbury, but Sunbury decided against this and became the 45th Middlesex Rifle Volunteer Corps. The Feltham and Staines combination was not a friendly success and Feltham moved towards Twickenham.

In 1860 the 44th was one of the Rifle Corps which were linked together to form the 7th (Admin) Battalion of the Middlesex Rifle Volunteers. Drill took place in the malthouse. The uniform was medium grey melton cloth with silver piping (white for rank and file). Complete with badge it cost £5 5s 6d (£5.27p.) Later the uniform was changed to dark grey with silver facings. It consisted of tunic, trousers, sloppy soft peaked cap, black leather belt with the usual snake fastener, black leather gaiters and rifle sling. The grey shako was taken into use and when the helmet was adopted the peaked cap was replaced by a grey pill box and the field service cap (fore and aft). The old shako plate was used on the helmet until stocks of the Middlesex Rifle Volunteers helmet plate became available. This consisted of the usual Maltese cross bearing a stringed bugle as the general motif. Staines 44th Rifle Volunteers however, had its own badge on the pouch. This consisted of the usual garter strap with 44th Middlesex Rifles thereon, surrounding a shield bearing three seaxes, the whole surmounted by an antique crown, in white metal. By the time that the regulation red tunic with yellow half patches on the collar had been generally adopted, the Staines men were part of the 55th/77th Regiment of Foot, the Middlesex Regiment. On the outbreak of the Boer War in 1899 the Volunteers from Staines were wearing the mauve-khaki slouch hat of the CIV (Civic Imperial Volunteers), the uniform then being khaki with leather accoutrements and puttees. Later, after the Territorial Army was formed in 1908 they returned to the red tunic, blue trousers and helmet and peaked forage cap.

Of the military families of Staines the Bone family were foremost, the first to join the 44th Middlesex Rifle Volunteers in 1857. One member of the family reached the rank of Colour Sergeant. At the outbreak of the Boer War, learning that the Militia were not to be sent out immediately, he joined the Civic Volunteers as a private as they were to be drafted earlier. He died of disease in South Africa.

Below right: Shako plate, The Middlesex Volunteers.
J. E. Smith

Below left: Badge of the 44th Rifle Volunteers. *J. E. Smith*

In January 1879 at the defence of Rourke's Drift in Natal during the Zulu War, Colour Sgt Bourne of the 24th Regiment of Foot (2nd Battalion Warwickshire Regiment) organised the defence of the outer perimeter. By his skill the men became a fighting unit which captured the imagination of the British public of that time and their record has become military history. Some of the men were awarded the VC. Colour Sgt Bourne received a Commendation and was granted an audience by Queen Victoria at Windsor Castle. He came to Staines as a musketry instructor to the Staines Rifle Volunteers (7th Admin Battalion, the Middlesex Regiment) c1895, and lived at No 4 Tilley's Lane. At the end of his tour of duty in Staines he returned to his native Birmingham, retired from the army and died about 1914.

In World War 1 the 10th Battalion was composed mainly of Staines and Hounslow men. This battalion was later, like many other territorial regiments, extended into the 1st, 2nd and 3rd line Battalions of the 10th Battalion. All three battalions fared very favourably. On 1 January 1917 the 1st/10th were in India, 2nd/10th in Egypt and the 3rd/10th in training were soon to be sent to the front in France. This was unusual as very few third battalions saw service abroad. After a fine fighting record, the 3rd/10th Battalion, although not disbanded as a fighting unit, ceased to exist on 23 February 1918 and became the 11th Entrenching Battalion. By 1919 men from the other line battalions were transferred to other units and demobilised. Some of the now seasoned troops became members of the 25th Garrison Battalion who went on to suffer hardships at Murmansk in the Siberian campaign.

Between the wars the Territorial Army lost some of its glamour. The uniform was the drab khaki ('all the sameness') and after the Great War men were sickened by the horrors of battle. In the 1930s, however, the TA went through a rebirth. Being a 'terrier' was a good way to obtain a cheap holiday with pay in those hard times. The foot battalions were gone and in their stead recruits were needed for the Royal Engineers, Royal Artillery, Royal Signals and other units to make up the territorial army divisions, but in spite of this Staines maintained its company of the Middlesex Regiment.

In 1939, unlike World War 1, men were called to the colours into the Middlesex Regiment battalions and not into TA battalions of a definite district pattern (like the 10th Battalion). The district pattern had been good for troop morale with men who knew each other serving together in one body, but many villages and small towns had been left with few men aged between 18 and 40 after local units had been wiped out in the war. From 1939 men of the Middlesex Regiment were not Middlesex men and men of Middlesex were in other infantry units. However, men from Middlesex won fresh honours wherever they were. The 1st Battalion, the Middlesex Regiment was scooped up by the Japanese army at the surrender of Hong Kong, but at Dunkirk the regiment fought a gallant rearguard action and many reached home although many were taken prisoner by the Germans. After the peace of 1945 the Middlesex Regiment went on to Korea.

From 1950 the TA went through changes when National Servicemen were obliged to serve in its ranks. This, however, was not a good courtship and was soon over when their National Service time expired. Some stayed on but thousands decided against it. The popular regiments and corps of the day were able to take the numbers they required and some even had a waiting list.

Staines never lacked local recruits. It had an Infantry Company at Leacroft, a REME section in the Staines Linoleum sports ground and a small RE unit with an HQ in Ashford Road, Laleham. During the years of recruiting before the army reorganisation took place Staines catchment area was justly able to boast of its Cadet Units. These were the Army Cadet Unit with HQ at the Drill Hall at Leacroft, the Sea Cadet Unit at TS Thamesis near Staines bridge, and the Air Training Corps in the Staines Linoleum sports field.[4]

Below: Laying up of colours, 75th Middlesex Army Cadet Corps. *J. Livermore collection*

Local Industry

In 19th century Staines, a variety of local industries and specialist trades were practiced including the following industries: bleaching, brewing, calico printing, candle factory, iron foundry, linoleum factory, milling, mustard manufacture, papier mache works, wharfingering. Specialist trades included: basketmakers*, boatbuilders (timber), carriers (by barge and horsedrawn vehicles), a carver and gilder, a coachbuilder, farriers, fishermen including eel catchers, reed cutters, saddlers, a stay maker, straw bonnet maker, truss maker, an umbrella maker, watch and clock makers. There were fewer gravel pits in the 19th century but more general agriculture and market gardening.

Below: The history of the supply of gas to Staines belongs to four companies: from 1833/4 the Staines & Egham Gas & Coke Co; which from 1915 was absorbed by Brentford Gas Co; in 1926 there was an amalgamation of companies into the Gas Light & Coke Co and in 1949 North Thames Gas took over. Illustrated is a bill from the Brentford Gas Company.

Perhaps the most interesting of the local industries was the Linoleum factory whose impact extended beyond the immediate Staines area.

The Linoleum Manufacturing Co Ltd
It was at Staines that a revolution in floor covering took place in the second half of the 19th century. At the beginning of the century 'floor-cloth' was commonly used. It had limited durable qualities, its patterns wore off and Frederick Walton's invention of linoleum was to supersede it. Walton was the son of a Yorkshire engineer who settled in Manchester. He moved to London and, having found by experiment a satisfactory way of making his new product, he looked around for suitable factory premises. By chance he found a disused

*Basket making had been a trade since the middle ages when reed baskets were made to carry produce to London markets and local markets — an early form of prepackaging. Basket making was carried on by at least one firm until the end of World War 2.

The Brentford Gas Company bill:

THE BRENTFORD GAS COMPAN

factory at Staines with water power (Hale Mill on
the River Colne) and several acres of land. The mill
had a large pair of rollers previously used by a
calico printing works, the most expensive part of
the equipment he needed. In 1864 the Linoleum
Manufacturing Co Ltd came into being. Running at
a loss for a few years, it gradually captured the
home and world markets. Judicious advertising
helped to bring success. For the first time durable
and attractive floor covering was available at prices
which could be afforded by the ordinary family, an
achievement of British technology the magnitude
of which has been forgotten today. Within 10 years
the Staines works covered 10-12 acres and by
1930 these had grown to 45 acres with improved
techniques and modern power sources.

In 1907 the White Star line was the first of the

Right: Hale Mill 1964. It has since been demolished.
Barry (Staines) Ltd

**Below: An aerial view of Staines taken in 1928. At left,
the GWR station and Wyrardisbury River form the
boundary of the extensive premises of Staines Linoleum
Co. Beyond the SR railway line is the area now occupied
by the Moormede estate.** *Aerofilms*

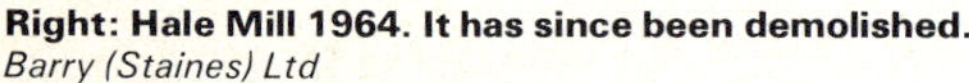

Above: The 1844 Quaker Meeting House, High Street.
Middlesex Chronicle

Right: The Oast House, Kingston Road, which was built between 1824 and 1851. Now an adult training centre it was originally part of the Harris brewing business bought out by the Ashby brewery 1903 and closed down.
Chris Leigh

Below right: The Malt House, Moor Lane, rear of 57 Church Street. Probably built by Thomas II Ashby, it was originally part of the only 19th century industrial complex surviving in Staines today (the Ashby Brewery, now Courage (Central) Ltd). *Chris Leigh*

great shipping lines to use linoleum generally. Others followed suit and it was used extensively in hospitals, large office blocks etc. This development meant steady employment for many in Staines where it became a major industry. The company was joined by a major Scottish company from Kirkcaldy to form the Barry (Staines) Group in 1930 (now called Barry (Staines) UK Ltd). Since then vinyl floorings have gradually competed strongly and the group has decreased in capacity. It moved away to High Wycombe some years ago and the old factory buildings and the mill were demolished about 1973 to make way for a new industrial complex.

'Staines Lino', as it was called locally, took the name of Staines round the world and had the distinction of creating a revolution in its field in

social history and is a landmark in the industrial history of Staines.

The Quakers in Staines

As in most Middlesex towns, so also in Staines, the Quakers played a large part in the commercial and educational development of the town. Their earliest recorded marriage is 1670, the birth registers start in 1671, but their meetings were at first in private houses in the 1650s. Their first Meeting House in Blackboy Lane was completed in 1715. In 1844 they opened a new building with a handsome frontage on to the High Street. Their membership dropped considerably between the two world wars and the meeting house was sold, the smaller community putting up with a temporary hut near their second cemetery behind the high Street in 1936 (the first burial ground was behind Stainton House in Church Street). The second cemetery was cleared in 1972 and the hut later removed to make way for the Elmsleigh Centre development. In 1975, after over 325 years in Staines, the Quakers moved to Egham.

Those well known and respected in their time included: Dr Pope, physician to George III and his daughter Princess Amelia. Dr Pope was renowned for his humane treatment of the mentally ill in an age when attitudes to such afflictions can only be described as cruel. His daughter, Margaret, was a great educationalist, founding and teaching in local schools which had pupils of families of all denominations. The library at Matthew Arnold Girls' School bears her name and books from her

Above: The brewery tower (1903) and rear of 57 Church Street.
Chris Leigh

Left: 57 Church Street where Thomas II Ashby started his brewing business in the kitchen.
Staines & Egham News

Charity are received annually. Partner to Dr Pope was Dr Tothill who name is remembered in Tothill Street which has only recently disappeared. Two other doctors were also of considerable standing, Dr Frederick and his son Dr Albert Curtis. The Finch family, owners of the mustard mill were a well established family in Staines before the arrival of the Ashbys.

The many members of the Ashby family were variously connected with a wharf, mills, the brewery in Church Street, the bank in the High Street (later Barclay's), ironmongery and wine vaults. The founder, the first Thomas Ashby, a mealman, came to Staines before 1757 as a comparatively poor man. He prospered and founded a large family. In the 3rd and 4th generations when Staines had a population of under 4,000 there were 16 Ashby households and 14 Mrs Ashbys. The last Ashby of Staines, John Ashby, gave the Ashby Recreation Ground (locally known as 'The Lammas') to the town in 1922. The history of the Ashbys in Staines is contained in Robert Ashby's book. John Ashby was JP for Middlesex County bench for 35 years; chairman of Spelthorne bench for over 20 years; first County Councillor from Staines for Middlesex (20 years); Deputy Lieutenant of the County of Middlesex; member of Staines UDC for 38 years and chairman for most of that time. Robert Ashby concludes by saying: '. . . the history of this family of Staines . . . is that of one rapidly developed and quickly rooted, and as rapidly uprooted and scattered.'

Top: The Quaker hut and burial ground. *Tony Keen*

Above: Corner Hall, at the corner of Church Street and Vicarage Road. It is reputed to have been built on the site of a leper burial ground c300 years ago and has later additions. It was sold in 1772 by Thomas and Sarah Finch (mustard mill family) to Thomas I Ashby. It remained in Ashby hands for over 120 years. The wistaria floribunda, one of several brought to England from Japan in the 1870s, was planted by Harry Day. *Mark Mitchell*

Left: Springfield/Moor House, Vicarage Road (east end). Built in 1867, it was sold in 1887 by Robert Ashby to Charles W. Finch who renamed it Moor House. It became the Staines Eventide Home in 1948 and is still known as Moor House.
Hist Soc collection

Religious Life in Staines

Top: St Mary's choir outside the Blue Anchor c1910.
Chris Leigh collection

Above: Church Street and St Mary's church tower. The house in front is Corner Hall. Inset is the London Stone (see page 25). *Middlesex Chronicle*

As well as the above connections with the Quakers, Staines has and has had a considerable variety of religious life. The Church of England is represented by the Parish Church — St Mary's — and St Peter's. The former, the Parish Church of St Mary the Virgin, Vicarage Road, stands on the site of older churches — the first recorded in 675AD — and the lower part of the brick tower dates from 1631-4. The present church was built in 1828 and since that date the only major alteration has been to the upper tower's embattled parapet and pinnacles of stone. These were removed c1950 after they became unsafe (attributed to the damage from a bomb falling in Wraysbury Road during World War 2) and at the same time the galleries were removed from the church's interior. Also of note in St Mary's are two stained glass windows: one dedicated to Abp Stephen Langton who was present with King John at Runnymede in 1215 and consecrated the bishops of St David's and Bangor in St Mary's; the second window was erected by the Kaiser in memory of Miss Byrne who was a nurse to his children when he was Crown Prince. She lived in one of the cottages in Binbury Row.

St Peter's Church in the Laleham Road was built of brick in the Victorian Gothic Revival style in 1893-4, mainly through the generosity of Sir Edward Clarke QC after whose family the bells are named.

Other denominations in Staines are, or have been, located at:

Church of Jesus Christ of Latter Day Saints, Kingston Road.
Baptist church (Church Street 1778-1810; Church Street 1824; Bridge Street 1837 to date).
Congregational Church (Tilley's Lane 1789, Thames Street 1837-1956; Kingston Road 1956 to date. The Boys Brigade was founded in 1923).
Methodist Church (in two small converted cottages, Kingston Road 1771; Kingston Road Church 1853, church on the other side of Kingston Road 1890 to date).
Roman Catholic Church of Our Lady of the Rosary, Gresham Road 1890, to date.
Salvation Army Citadel, Kingston Road (in former Methodist Hall, Kingston Road 1892; New Citadel 1953 to date). The Salvation Army Band was formed in 1891/2.
Synagogue (room in High Street 1943; Synagogue in Tothill Street 1953, which moved to South Street in 1975)
The First Church of Christ Scientist, Cherry Orchard.
Jehovah Witness, Chestnut Grove (Blue Ribbon Gospel Army c1882).
The Society of Friends (Quakers), Staines 1660-1973 (now 'of Egham and Staines') Limes Road, Egham 1973 to date.

Below: Interior of St Peter's church. *Chris Leigh collection*

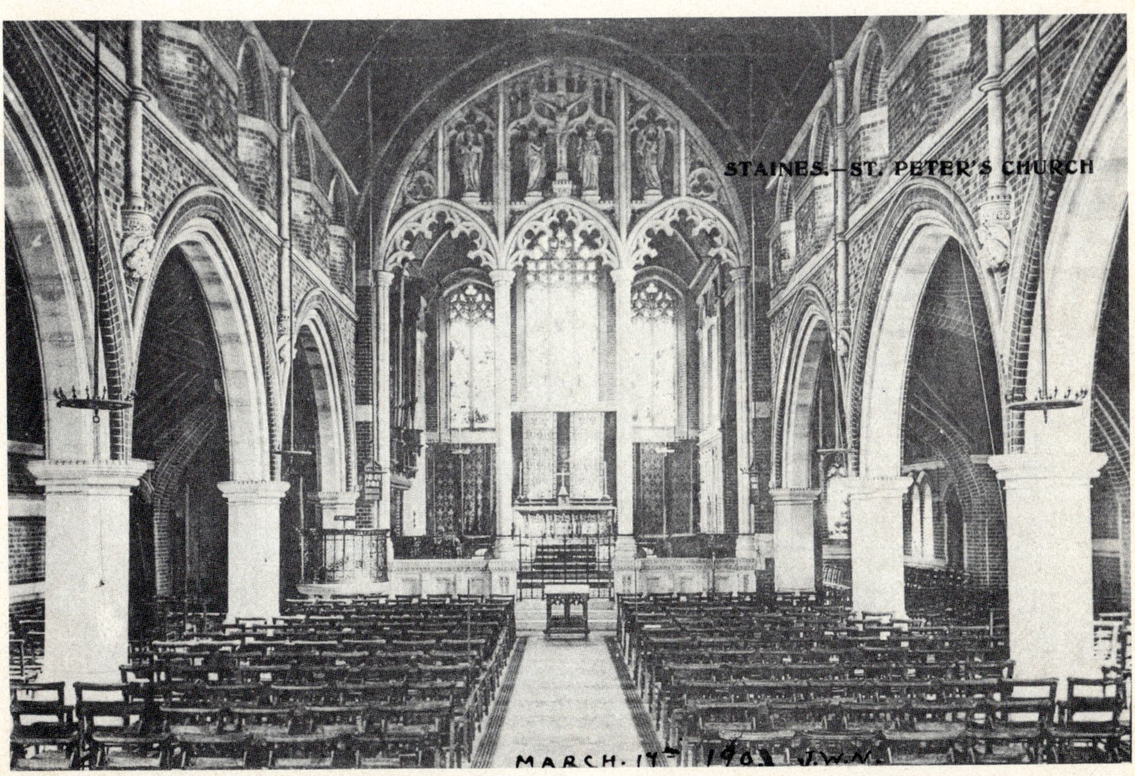

Above: St Peter's church from the river.
Middlesex Chronicle

Below: The simple elegance of St Mary's church, dominated by its tower (rebuilt 1828) reputedly designed by 17th century architect Inigo Jones. A 1900 view.
Chris Leigh

Right: St Peter's church seen from the river on a misty day in 1980. *Chris Leigh*

The Thames at Staines

As with all riverside towns, Staines was built up around the Thames' mercantile potential. An artery of transport, the trade on the river enabled the town to grow in size. The management of rivers was a royal perogative until 1350, but rights over the Thames were sold by Richard I to the Corporation of the City of London in 1197. The London Stone marks the limit of the City's jurisdiction. The date on the stone, 1285, indicates when the ancient stone was set up there. It has been the scene of various visits of the Lords Mayor and of 'bumping' ceremonies for new watermen at swan upping time.

Control of navigation was a great problem for many years. Various commissions were set up and some pound locks were built, but no great advance was made until the Thames Conservancy came into being in 1857. The City of London then lost all control over the Thames but was represented on the Board. The Conservancy became responsible for the river from Staines down to the Nore and, from 1866, up to Cricklade. The Port of London Authority came into being in 1908 and took over the stretch from Teddington down to the Nore. The Conservancy solved the traffic problem by building locks and dredging the river bed which resulted in the control and containment of the flow of the river.

It was, however, too late for the commercial traffic because of the competition from the roads and later the railways. Certain traffic survived, the carrying of coal by barge to the gas works and of timber to destinations higher up the river, but even these had ceased by the 1930s. The main benefit from improved navigation was for pleasure boats.

The most important work of the Conservancy and of its successor, the Thames Water Authority, over the last 25 years has been the successful fight against pollution. In the early 1920s it was possible to look down from Staines Bridge through clear water to the river bed beneath. Today, although the water does not look so clear the Thames is considered to be a clean river.

The major importance of the Thames is the supply of drinking water for London and its suburbs. However the use of the Thames for recreational pursuits is a more obvious blessing. As a pleasure area the Thames at Staines became of importance around the 1880s. Bank holidays and Sundays saw it crowded with small craft. The wealthier people owned their own boats which they kept at boatyards along the river. When they went on the river they took picnic fare of lavish proportions with them. Before 1914 some of them formed clubs, eg the Neleus which used the small

Right: Feeding hungry swans during the floods of 1964.
Middlesex Chronicle

Below: The Thames Conservancy. This device with the words 'Conservators of the River Thames' within the roundel's circle was on the iron boundary marks to the rear of the towpath. (One can still be seen on the Staines reach.)

Top: Swan Upping: the Queen's Swanmaster's skiff.
Middlesex Chronicle

Above: Swan Upping: preparing to catch the cygnets.
Middlesex Chronicle

Right: John Tims' boatyard behind Church Island c1912.
Author's collection

boathouse at Biffens as their clubhouse. After a day
on the river they returned for a picnic supper.
Members had furnished and carpeted the
clubhouse comfortably and gas was laid on for
heating and lighting. Founded by John Rourke it
was principally a social club with a membership of
about 40. Some came from Ealing but there were
local members as well, a number of whom kept
their boats there. Their clubhouse reverted to an
ordinary workshop about 60 years ago.

There were also many who owned or rented
riverside bungalows for the summer season, many
of them stage personalities. As late as the early
1920s the author can remember Gordon Selfridge
had a small bungalow on the reach below the
railway bridge. When he went on the river a
marvellous ritual took place: the French windows
were opened with a flourish and two footmen
solemnly processed down the lawn to the launch
carrying a picnic basket and rugs. Then Selfridge's
mother would be wheeled down in an invalid chair
and ensconced in the launch and off she and her
son would go for a picnic on the river. This always
seemed to be an echo of grandeur of days gone by,
but after all he could afford it and it certainly made
quite a spectacle for the onlooker on the opposite
bank. As the bungalow was quite small, certainly
not big enough to accommodate staff, perhaps it
was only used in the day time with Selfridge and
his mother returning to London at the end of the
day by car.

The working man's holidays in the early days
were bank holidays and Sundays and the river
became popular because it was easy and cheap to
reach from London either by bus or train. Although
they had little boat skill, having no opportunity for
practice, they had a respect for property, in contrast
to today, and were careful of the boats they hired.
Those better endowed and more skilful in
watermanship referred to them rather unkindly as
'the braces brigade'. However, they were a good
natured lot and it must have been a wonderful
experience for them in those days of long working
hours and little leisure. Even as late as the
beginning of the 1920s the river was so popular at
weekends and on holidays that between the two
bridges at Staines, the river was so full of craft that
one could almost have walked on boats from one
side of the river to the other.

All this was to change dramatically when there
was a decline in river popularity. The Empire
Exhibition at Wembley in 1924 (which maybe
outshone the Great Exhibition at the Crystal Palace
of 1851) drew enormous crowds and there were
some who maintained this to be a contributory
factor to the decline, but there were also two other
factors. The arrival of cheap motor cars on the
market enabled many to go further afield and off
the bus and train routes, and petrol was very cheap.
There was also the social change in holidays for

working people which enabled them to take more
than one day at a time away from work. During
World War 2 it was still possible to go out on the
river, predominantly in hand propelled craft owing
to petrol rationing, but as soon as the war was over
the river began to come into its own again. First of
all the number of houseboats of varying kinds was
noticeable, converted lifeboats, converted landing
craft, cruisers, anything that would provide a home
during the acute housing shortage of the
immediate post war era. Once petrol rationing
came to an end boating became more mobile.
Motor boats of all kinds from the small boat with
outboard to cruisers of varying sizes became
increasingly popular and many were privately
owned. Fleets of hire cruisers were gradually built
up as demand grew and are now big business.

Serving the river enthusiasts were the
boatyards. John Tims and Sons' large boathouses
below the railway bridge covered a variety of
business, boat building, letting of small craft, and
later the hiring of launches and cruisers. They also
had a small boathouse behind Church Island which
they gave up about 1928.

George H. Beedell had a small boat hiring
business just above the railway bridge and on his
fascia board was written 'Under the Patronage of
HIH the Grand Duke Michael of Russia', perhaps
this was a counterblast to Tims' 'By Appointment'
British royal coat of arms. Beedell's closed down in
the late 1920s.

Biffens, above Staines Bridge, founded in 1880
by W. Snelson, was a medium sized boat business,
building and letting small craft. It later had some
motor boats for hire as well. The firm's boathouses
were built in the old river bed (now filled in). The
Thames originally divided into several necks of
water above Staines bridge and as late as 1891 it
was possible to row a skiff up from the Hythe
cottages to the rear of Biffens Boathouse. This
piece of water was originally the main river and
became the county boundary between Middlesex
and Surrey and as it dried up it became the county
ditch. It meandered behind the towpath and at a
varying distance inland until it met the mainstream
and a third county boundary, that of
Buckinghamshire, at the bungalow Counties' End.
This boundary, incomprehensible to many
nowadays, creates a strip of land belonging to
Staines which would reasonably be expected to
belong to Egham. One member of Biffens spent
most of World War 2 at Chertsey building motor
torpedo boats and fire tenders and also prepared
private craft which took part in the evacuation of
Dunkirk. The business now trades as Cheesman,
Rollo & Co. Its present business covers hiring of
cruisers and the building of and fitting out of
fibreglass cruisers for hire fleets at home and
abroad.

Another boatyard was that of Tom Taylor &

Sons. The works were founded in 1901 and were located above Staines bridge to the rear of the Ship Inn. They were builders mainly of motor boats. They also had a boatyard beside the Bridge House Hotel which Tom Taylor also owned for a time. They hired out small craft, motor launches and electric canoes. Small steamers were also built in this yard. It continued a letting trade until 1938 when the building of the ABC Cinema had begun on the site of the Bridge House Hotel in Clarence Street. The works on the Surrey side of the river continued under the same name, directed by the sons Jim and later Jack Taylor whose niece sold the works to Cars, Cranes & Slings Ltd in April 1980.

Regattas

Staines had three: the Staines Amateur Regatta, founded 1850, is still an annual event held in July on the reach between the railway bridge and the Fishing Temple. This was the first regatta after Henley to introduce races for eights in its programme.[5] The Staines & Egham Waterman's

Sport in Staines

The River Thames has provided a major amenity for sportsmen and women in Staines. But the town also offers its inhabitants a number of other sporting facilities including association and rugby football, cricket, hockey and tennis clubs — as well as many others too numerous to illustrate.

STAINES AMATEUR REGATTA, 1874.

Stewards,

His Grace the Duke of Leeds	Lewis Paine, Esq.	C. W. Finch, Esq.
Sir John Gibbons, Bart.	R. F. Wilkins, Esq.	Lord Henry Lennox
Thomas Wood, Esq.	Lord George Hamilton, M.P.	Sir Mordaunt W. Wells,
Leeds Paine, Esq.	George Cubitt, Esq., M.P.	Arthur Finch, Esq.
Lord Strafford	Thomas Ashby, Esq.	F. W. Ashby, Esq.
Sir Robert B. Harvey, Bart.		

Committee of Management,

T. R. Bixon, Esq.	John Adams, Esq.	Howard Fowler, Esq.
A. Frampton, Esq.	A. W. Bixon, Esq.	W. Wallace, Esq.
F. T. Ashby, Esq.	John Ashby, Esq.	Richard Ashby, Esq.
	Thomas Ashby, Esq., Jun.	

THIS REGATTA WILL BE HELD

On Thursday, July 23rd, 1874,

OPEN TO GENTLEMEN AMATEURS ONLY,

When the following Races will take place for

VALUABLE PRIZES.

THE STAINES CHALLENGE EIGHTS.

A SILVER PLATE, VALUE 40 GUINEAS, WITH PRESENTATION PRIZES,

To be competed for by those who have never won an Eight-oared Race.

(Now held by the Thames Rowing Club.)

Entrance Fee, £1 4/-

THE LADIES' CHALLENGE PLATE, VALUE 25 GUINEAS,

WITH PRESENTATION PRIZES

(Now held by the Molesey Rowing Club.)

For Four-oared Boats .... Entrance Fee, £2 10/-

FOUR-OARS, *SENIORS* .... Entrance Fee, £3 3/-

FOUR-OARS, *JUNIORS* .... Entrance Fee, £2 12/6

A CANOE RACE FOR THE CHALLENGE PADDLE,

A Valuable Silver Plate, to become the Property of the Competitor who may win it for three consecutive years.

(Now held by Mr. G. Knowles, one year)

WITH PRESENTATION PRIZE. Entrance Fee, £1 1/-

SCULLS, *SENIORS* .... Entrance Fee, £1 1/-

SCULLS, *JUNIORS* .... Entrance Fee, 15/6.

PAIR-OARS .... Entrance Fee, £2 2/-

SCRATCH RACES .... Entrance Fee, 6/-

TWO MILITARY BANDS WILL BE IN ATTENDANCE.

N.B.—All Coxswains weighing less than eight stone, will be required to carry weight on their thwarts, to make up the deficiency, and provide their own weights. (Coxswains weighed out after the races.)

Competitors are particularly requested to carry a Conspicuous Flag in their boat, so that their Color can be easily distinguished.

THE COMMITTEE RESERVE TO THEMSELVES THE RIGHT TO REFUSE ANY ENTRY.

FRANCIS T. ASHBY, (STAINES,)

HON. SECRETARY.

[P.T.O.

Above: A facsimile of the 1874 Staines Amateur Regatta programme cover.

Left: Views of the 1938 Thames Punting Championship — the Men's 2ft Punting Handicap (not a championship race) and the Ladies Thames Open Punting Championship race.
Sport and General

Right: Views of the 1981 Staines Regatta. *Middlesex Chronicle*

Regatta, founded in 1891, attracted entries from professional watermen from all reaches of the river. There were both rowing and sculling events, punting and also some more light hearted events towards the end of the day sometimes ending with a procession of illuminated boats after dark. Its last regatta was held in 1930. About the same time the last Childrens Regatta was held. This was a very popular local event which was held in the backwater between the banks of the Lammas and the upstream end of Church Island. A spectacular firework display was always held after this regatta. The fireworks were mounted on Church Island and it always seemed that most of the population of Staines as well as visitors gathered on the Lammas to watch them.

Boat Clubs

The Staines Boat Club's premises are within the boundaries of Egham. It was founded in 1851 and totally destroyed by fire in 1950. The present building is on a site some yards further away from the railway bridge. The town of Egham is 'twinned' with the French town of Joinville le Pont. Members of the French club, le Societé Nautique de la Marne, compete at the Staines Amateur Regatta and are entertained by members of the Staines Boat Club. On the morning after the regatta a farewell party is held in the clubhouse and some hilarious

impromptu races take place between the two clubs. Strode's College Boat Club is nearby, between the Railway Bridge and Tims' boathouses.

Staines Town Rowing Club, founded 1920 and originally professional, housed its boats at the Swan, Egham Hythe. It was moved to Laleham where it became the Burway Rowing Club and is now a flourishing club. The Thames Punting Club has held its Championship Meetings at Staines from time to time.

Swimming

The Ashby Recreation Ground provides facilities for swimming in the Thames and also has a young

Right: Staines Bridge and Biffens boatyard c1938. *Author's collection*

Below: 'Wag' or 'Otter' hone making an eel pot in the 1920s. Tom Taylor's Bridge House boatyard can be seen in the background. *Author's collection*

children's paddling pool. There was at one time a swimming club on the upstream end of Church Island, but this ceased in the late 1920s.

Fishing

When the Thames was quieter with few motor boats there were several professional fishermen, owners of fishing punts, who would take their customers out and moor where there was a good 'swim'. This made a pleasant day for the fishing enthusiast. 'Wag' Hone was probably the last of these professionals. He was also an eel catcher and made his own eel pots, and was for some years the publican of the Farmer's Inn in the Hythe, Egham.

Today, fishermen can still be seen along the banks of the river, and fishing clubs come down for annual competitions. The profusion of fish varies from season to season for a variety of reasons, but over many years coarse fish have included roach, dace, bream, pike and barbel. Trout have, within living memory, been almost non-existent except in the upper reaches of the Thames, although on one occasion at Staines in the 1940s a trout jumped into the lap of a startled lady sitting in a punt. She took it to the Swan in the Hythe where it was cooked for her supper. Salmon once abounded in the Thames and there is a record of payment in 1530 to some Staines men by Henry VIII for supplying salmon.

Swan Upping

The ceremony of swan upping[6] is 400-500 years old and takes place about the third week of July when the cygnets are some six weeks old. The route is from Vintry Wharf, London, to Henley. Upping is a form of stocktaking by the three owners of games of swans. All free flying and unmarked swans are the property of the Crown. The Vintners Company's swans are pinioned and are marked with a nick on each side of the upper beak, and the Dyers Company's swans are also pinioned and marked with one nick on the right side of the upper beak. The three swanmasters have two skiffs apiece manned by Thames watermen. The cavalcade of boats can be seen on the Staines reach between the bridges on the second day at about 9.45am. Anyone wishing to watch this ancient and unique ceremony should, near the due time, ask a Thames lock keeper on what day the uppers are to be expected.

Swans mate for life and live to about 40 years old. They are now reduced in numbers owing to the decrease in natural food, like ribbon weed, lead poisoning and lack of peaceful nesting places. They also have acute food problems at times of flood and severe frost or snow when the swanmasters supply them with bread and corn in an attempt to save them from death from starvation.

Left: The wharf behind Church Island during the floods of 1891. *Hist Soc collection*

Below left: Belle View, Riverside. In its day Belle View was a fine example of the larger important suburban house with fairly extensive grounds. The decoration above the french bow windows can also be seen on buildings of the same period in the town. It was demolished in 1979. *Staines & Egham News*

Below: Return from walking the dog in Counties' End garden during the floods of 1927. *Author's collection*

Right: The London Stone (photo c1900). The ancient stone was placed on the pedestal in 1280 with the words 'God Bless ye Cittye of London'. The names of several Lords Mayor are also inscribed. The last Lord Mayor's visit was on 17 July 1957. *Author's collection*

Below: Looking upstream from the ferry landing adjacent to the Pack Horse Hotel, with the punt ferry crossing to the Surrey Bank. *B. Ashworth collection*

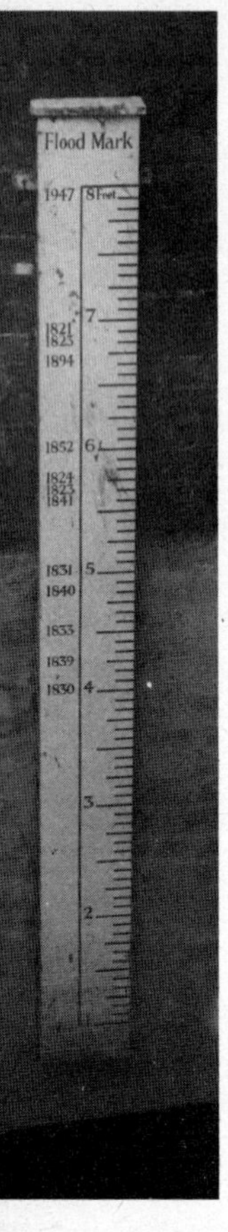

Far left: The flood board. Positioned on a wall above the River Colne, Church Street, the flood board is not accurate but gives an idea of the frequency of heavy floods in the area in the past. Winter and spring floods were common up to the 1960s. The 1947 flood was the result of exceptional conditions: a very hard frost followed by snow. The hard frozen ground could not absorb any of the sudden thaw of snow which followed and which all therefore went direct into the river. The flood at its peak was 6ft 3in above normal level (5in lower than the 1894 flood and not as shown on the board). In 1894 the late C. R. Smithers went by water in a punt from Tims' boatyard in Chertsey Lane to Thorpe! *Chris Leigh*

Left: The rollers under the railway bridge. When the railway bridge was built 1855/6, three vertical rollers were attached to the lower part of the buttresses on the towpath. These prevented the towropes of the barges from fraying when they touched the buttresses (which was unavoidable) and also prevented damage to the buttresses by wear. In the earliest days of barge traffic the river was wider and more shallow and the millers of Staines used to divert water from the river by means of flash weirs and sluices to run their mills. This often meant that there was not enough water for the barges with the result that they had to tie up and await the millers' pleasure. The waiting sometimes lasted for days and the men who were towing had to kick their heels. Boredom then led to fights among themselves and also with the local citizens. This became quite a scandal and was a strong argument in favour of having the river's flow better controlled by locks, weirs and dredging.
Chris Leigh

Right: The 'Hook On' and 'Shoot Off' cottages are probably 150–200 years old and are a link with the days when barge traffic on the river was a common sight. Until about the end of the 18th century, barges were pulled by teams of men, but by the 19th century teams of horses were used. Coming upstream, before the barge reached the cottages, the horses were whipped up Thames Street and the towrope was taken off (which needed accurate timing) and the barge carried on under its own 'way' to the other side of the river where it was tied up until the horses were hooked on again. The horses were either ferried across the river or taken through the town, over the bridge and down the towpath on the other side. If the barge had to tie up below the cottages to off-load or to stay overnight it was necessary to float a rope down to the barge to tow it across. At one time there was a man with his own team of horses who earned his living doing this. Going downstream the whole process could be carried out by shooting off the rope and letting the stream carry the barge across to the other side. There is a bollard by the public slipway between the cottages and the railway bridge which was used by the bargemen when they tied up there. *Chris Leigh*

Left: In 1887 there were 257 Coal Duties boundary marks recorded for maintenance. Of these 220 have been traced in the past 20 years, but some have now disappeared. They were set up under the London Coal and Wine Duties Continuance Act of 22 July 1861 along the boundary of the Metropolitan police district to mark an area within which the Corporation of the City of London was empowered to collect duties on coal entering the area. There are five different types in metal or stone. A cast iron post stands on the Staines/Egham border near The Hythe, another in the hedge opposite by the path leading to the river, and a third outside 'Counties' End' bungalow on the towpath near River Park Avenue. These are painted white with the cross of St George in red and the sword of St Paul and '24 & 25 Vict Cap 42' in black. A tall obelisk is on the embankment by the railway bridge in Thames Street. The London Stone was also used as a marker. Any coal entering the Port of London or Westminster or passing over the Metropolitan police boundary into London by water, road, or (latterly) by railway paid the duties. Originally the duties were intended to pay for the rebuilding of London after the Great Fire of 1666 including the rebuilding of St Paul's between 1675 and 1710. Coal duties authorised by later Acts were used for improving London by creating new streets and widening existing ones and also helped the Corporation of the City of London to free itself from debt by 1834. In 1862 authority to collect the duties was transferred to the forerunner of London CC, namely the Metropolitan Board of Works which built the three London Thames embankments, Northumberland Avenue, Hyde Park Corner and Holborn Viaduct which was the first London flyover. A Continuance Act of 1868 paid off a loan raised to free Staines Bridge from tolls in 1871. All duties ceased on 5 July 1890.
Chris Leigh (Information from Maurice Bawtry)

Right: The Literary & Scientific Institute, on the corner of Clarence Street and Bridge Street and built specifically for this purpose. The foundation stone was laid in 1835 by the Rt Hon Sir W. H. Fremantle. Among recorded lecturers was H. G. Wells. The trustees and members of committee were composed of men of local prominence including Quakers. When the last trustee, Mr Pownall, died the property which was copyhold, reverted to Henry Fladgate who sold it to John Ashby. A printing business was in occupation in 1916. Later for some years it was an antique furniture shop which closed down in 1938/9. It was converted into a strongpoint to defend the bridge in 1939. Middlesex CC took it over as a county library c1948, this being the first public library in Staines. Surrey CC took it over with the merging of the counties. The library moved to the Oast House in Kingston Road in 1979.
Staines & Egham News

Staines' Bridges

No one can enter or leave Staines without crossing water. The Roman name Pontes, literally bridges, described Staines in their day as accurately as it would today. Bridges over the Thames have been many. Remains of a Roman bridge and wharf were discovered in 1980. The first recorded bridge was built of timber[7] from the market sqaure to below the Swan on the Surrey side. (This was the only bridge above London Bridge until a licence to build a bridge at Chertsey was granted in 1410.) The timber bridge had a long history. It was pulled down or perhaps partially cut during the Civil War when a ferry replaced it, but it was rebuilt in 1683 and survived until 1808. Staines bridges over the Thames were maintained by pontage or tolls levied on those passing over or under them. A three-span stone bridge designed by Thomas Sandby was opened in 1797 but part of it subsided within months. One of the approaches to it can still be seen in a wall near the Swan. In 1803 a single-span cast iron bridge designed by Thomas Paine was opened and almost immediately was a failure.[8] It seems odd that neither Sandby nor Paine were

qualified to design bridges. In 1807 the iron bridge having become badly cracked, was shored up with timber supports which made several arches. It continued, a hazard to navigation, until 1832.

In 1828 an Act authorised the building of a new bridge. This was designed by John and George Rennie, sons of the famous John Rennie who designed the old London bridge and many others. They chose a site some 300 yards further upstream. It was opened by George IV and Queen Adelaide. It was financed by private subscription as was usual then, and the investors lost on the deal.[9] The 1832 bridge has stood the test of time. Designed for, and originally carrying a notice stating 'Load not to exceed 10 tons', it rests on its original timber piles in the river bed. The only repair to its foundations was about 1910 when two bargeloads of clay were dropped round the pier on the Staines side.[10] Five Churchill tanks were seen stationary on it during the last war, a dead weight load of over 112 tons which it bore without complaint. It carries a heavy load of traffic today at any one time. Widened in 1958/9, the added weight involved does not seem to have affected adversely its robust construction.

The iron railway bridge further downstream was built to carry the Staines to Reading (LSWR) line

Below: Thomas Sandby's bridge completed with the old wooden bridge beyond it; from an old print.
J. Orr collection

Above: The Railway Bridge in the
winter of 1964/5. Staines Boat
Club is beyond the left hand
arch. *Middlesex Chronicle*

Left: Thomas Paine's bridge from
the river. *Middlesex Chronicle*

Below: Approach to Thomas
Paine's bridge from the market
square. *Middlesex Chronicle*

STAINES BRIDGE & BUSH INN. 1828

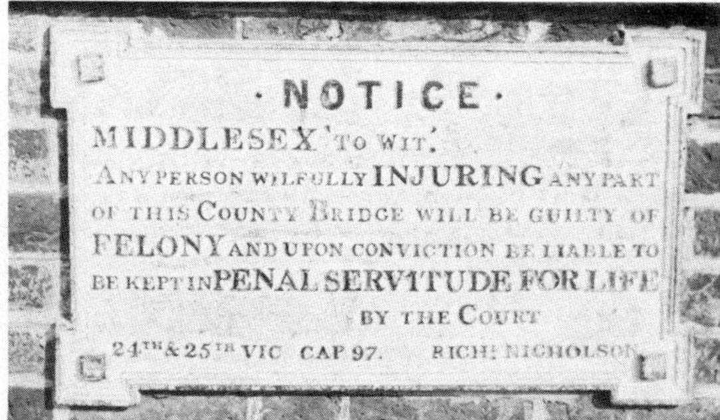

The 'Bailey' bridge built upstream from Staines bridge in 1939 was a wartime measure to carry anticipated increased military traffic and perhaps to be used as an alternative if the main bridge should be damaged. Its approaches were near the Ship Inn on the Egham side and just below the junction of Bridge Street and Clarence Street on the Staines side. It was reduced to a pedestrian only bridge after the war and finally completely removed in 1959. Many of the timbers were cut up into manageable pieces and dropped into the river. One of the workmen engaged on this task sat on a piece he was busily sawing through, but he was sitting on the piece to be sawn off. He was warned just in time before he too would have gone hurtling down on the piece he had cut!

which was opened in 1856. It is purely ultilitarian and cannot be described as one of the beauties of railway architecture.

Top: The Rennie bridge.
Middlesex Chronicle

Above: This notice dated 1861 was on the approach parapet to Staines Bridge (Surrey side) and was removed when repairs were carried out c1935. The Act quoted amends an Act of George IV wherein the penalty was deportation for life.
Hist Soc collection

Right: The Callender-Hamilton bridge, built in 1941, changed to pedestrians only in 1947 and was demolished in 1959.
Author's collection

Transport then and now

Coaching Days

Between the 18th and 19th centuries the increasing amount of horse-drawn traffic through Staines must have made it a very noisy place. The coming of the railways in 1848 (LSWR) and 1884 (GWR) brought a gradual reduction of coach traffic, but local horse-drawn vehicles, particularly of tradesmen, continued in use even up to the late 1920s in many cases. The coaching trade created much contingent trade in Staines and the number of horses it was necessary to have ready for changes at coaching inns must have been considerable. For example, at one time the Angel (& Crown) had six ostlers and 120 horses and additional stabling to the rear of the Thames Street corner of the present Johnson & Clarke's store. The Bush Inn had stabling for upward of 100 horses, the Red Lion for 20 in 1830 and the Bush & Clarence had a livery stable from 1832 to the 1850s.

There were three types of stage coaches: first appearing in the mid-17th century were coaches plying on long haul or fairly long haul routes. These were often owned by partnerships or hired by them from coachbuilders. There were also short journey coaches and Mail coaches. The first Mail coaches in 1784 were ordinary commercial coaches with a reduced number of passengers. Priority was given to the Mail rather than to the passengers and there was an armed guard. (A certain amount of mail had been carried by postboy on horseback since Elizabethan times.) By 1836 Mail coaches were specially built for and owned by the Post Office. Three regular Mail coaches went through the town each way daily, London to Poole, London to Penzance and London to Exeter. On Wednesdays the Exeter coach was known as an 'auxiliary coach' and carried foreign mail for Lisbon during the Napoleonic wars. The mail was sent to Falmouth where it was put on Post Office packet boats to Lisbon. Mail for Windsor was taken off at Staines and despatched by postboy on horseback twice daily. When George III was resident at Windsor this mail included a bottle of sea water sent up from Weymouth for him daily presumably for him to drink on medical advice.[11]

In addition to six Mail coaches through Staines daily (three each way), there were 38 regular commercial long distance and medium distance coaches daily (19 each way) making a total of 44 regular coaches through each day and, from 1851 a daily return horse-drawn bus between London and Staines.[11] Brayley in a *History of Surrey* stated that 80 or 90 coaches passed or repassed daily through Egham High Street. Staines probably had as many, as its total would have included a

Below: Ascot traffic, Staines Bridge 1851.
Middlesex Chronicle

miscellaneous number of coaches plying on a non-daily basis and there were, of course, a large number of additional coaches both private and commercial on days when there was racing at Runnymede and Ascot. Local traffic included tradesmen's vans and delivery carts, farmers carts, private vehicles of doctors and prominent men of the town and some on horseback. Traffic from outside the area included, by 1828, privately owned mail phaetons (built similarly to Mail coaches); coaches or 'drags' (four-in-hands) on long distance runs and owned by gentry who gloried in the skill of driving them; privately owned curricles, a fairly light vehicle with two horses, but sometimes four which became popular in the early years of the 19th century.[12] and travellers on horseback. Gypsy caravans were also part of this busy scene, the town well known to them, both on their travels, and for the annual fair[13] held in the High Street in front of what is now Debenham's store.

Apart from those employed in the hotel and catering trade as we would call it today, many people in Staines must have been employed in serving this travelling public as ostlers, farriers, harness makers and the like. The town had its own coachbuilder, William Carpenter, whose premises were in the High Street near the White Lion. He was coachbuilder to the Queen (Victoria), the Prince of Wales, Prince Christian and the Khedive of Egypt.[14] His business was sold out of the family about 1886 but continued until about 1918. The Carpenters lived at Hythe End House, The Hythe, across the river and their coachhouse was converted some years ago to a dwelling house called The Cottage.

The Railways
Chris Leigh

During the middle years of the 19th century, when the mania for promoting new railway lines was at its height, there were proposals for an astonishing number of schemes to serve Staines. The town was situated in the 'no man's land' between the GWR main line from London via Slough and Reading to Bristol, and the South Western Railway's (SWR) London-Southampton line via Woking. In addition there was an SWR line from London to Richmond, which offered an ideal choice for extension to Staines. In 1845 some six different railway plans covering the area between Staines and Wokingham were deposited with Parliament. Of these, one was a proposal for a Reading-Reigate line, which eventually resulted in the South Eastern Railway line from Ash through Wokingham to Reading. At the same time there were plans for a branch from the main line at Weybridge, through Chertsey to a terminus adjacent to Staines Bridge by the present 'Petters' roundabout.

In 1847 the Windsor, Staines & South Western

Top: Ascot coach 1904. *Middlesex Chronicle*

Above: Ascot traffic 1912 — brake with hackney licence plate. *Hist Soc collection*

Below: Push-pull train leaving the GWR station. To rear of train is the station house. *Middlesex Chronicle*

Above: Push–pull train arriving at the GWR station.
Middlesex Chronicle

Left: GWR station on the day of the closure, 27 March 1965. *Chris Leigh*

Railway was authorised from Richmond-Windsor with a branch from Staines to Wokingham. Both these lines were to be virtually on the present route. In 1851 the Staines & Woking Railway was proposed, with a line via Egham and Virginia Water. Next year, the present line was promoted as the Staines, Woking & Wokingham Junction Railway with James Rendell and John Gardiner as engineers. Tenders for the construction were accepted from a Mr McCormick and for the stations and ancilliary buildings from Oades & Son. In 1855 John Hawkshaw replaced Gardiner as Engineer, and set about improving the layout of the curved junctions at Staines and Wokingham. At this time he also received local protests that the pier of the river bridge at Staines projected into the Laleham Road. Little seems to have been done about this, and even today the road is narrow at this point.

The line to Windsor was opened as far as Datchet in 1848, and on 4 June 1856 the Staines-Ascot line was opened to traffic. The first through trains to Reading operated a month later, on 9 July 1856. The line was leased to the LSWR in 1858 and absorbed by them some 20 years later. In 1866 the LSWR completed its extension from Chertsey to Virginia Water (known as Knowle) and improvements were made to the line between there and Staines.

Various schemes were then put forward for railways linking West Drayton with Woking via Staines, one of these involving a junction with the LSWR Windsor line on Staines Moor. These led eventually to the construction of the Staines & West Drayton Railway, which opened in 1885 using its separate terminus in Moor Lane, Staines. It was worked from the outset by the GWR, being absorbed by them in 1900. Initially there was an intermediate station at Colnbrook only, but in 1895 a station was opened on Staines Moor to serve the Metropolitan Rifle Range which had been established there.

On the LSWR lines, stations were provided at all the places served today except Longcross, where a halt was opened to serve military extablishments in 1942. For a short period there was a station at Staines High Street, adjacent to Factory Path. This was doubtless prompted by the poor siting of the Staines Junction station which later became known optimistically as Staines Central and is now the town's only passenger station. Electric trains first operated through Staines to Windsor on 6 July 1930 and to Reading on 2 July 1939.

In 1939 a connecting line was laid on Staines Moor to link the GWR Staines-West Drayton

Above: Staines GWR station house. Originally called Moor House, it was also known locally as the Mill House. Built in 1820 with additions in 1850 and 1885, John Finch sold it and the mustard mill to the Staines & West Drayton Railway Co in about 1883. It became the station house with very little alteration and the mill was pulled down to make way for the side platform and yard. *K. A. Jaggers*

Right: The line from West Drayton to Staines West (GWR) was never more than a rural branch line and for most of its days was worked by a single engine and carriage known as the 'push-pull'. It always worked 'engine-first' to Staines and pushed its carriage on the return journey. In this 1950 view No 1443 approaches the top of the 1 in 175 climb from Yeoveney halt on Staines Moor. *D. Sutton collection/Ian Allan Library*

Below right: Floods were not uncommon in Moor Lane and this view of the GWR station and Mansbridge's Crushing and Grinding Mill (vacant and being offered to let by the Water Company) during World War 1 is typical. *Chris Leigh collection*

branch with the Southern Staines-Windsor lines. This was part of a scheme to provide diversionary routes by which freight trains might avoid London during the blitz. After the war the line was disused but a scheme to ressurrect it was put forward in 1960. It was felt that trains from West Drayton could be diverted over the wartime spur into Staines Central, thereby enabling closure of Staines West and eliminating the need for a bridge to carry the A30 Staines by-pass over the line. Short notice, and strong local opposition, led to the scheme being abandoned.

In the event, Staines West lost its passenger services in 1965 under the proposals of the Beeching Report. Crowds of spectators watched the last train leave on 27 March 1965 to the accompaniment of exploding detonators and carrying a placard proclaiming, 'The end is nigh, prepare to meet thy bus. Born 1885, died 1965, it's over, The end'. The line was then used only by freight trains serving an oil depot at Staines. In 1980 work commenced on connecting the oil depot sidings to the Southern lines because the

Above: Staines Central in 1963 showing the entrance porch which has since been demolished. *G. Biddle*

Below: A view of Staines Central station of the London & South Western Railway in the early years of the present century, with an 'up' train for Waterloo approaching. The down platform buildings were rebuilt in the 1930s.
B. Ashworth collection

track bed of the old GWR branch was required for the M25 motorway. So the very last train from West Drayton to Staines, a special excursion from Paddington, ran on 24 January 1981 poignantly carrying the placard which had adorned the 1965 train. Immediately afterwards the track across Staines Moor was torn up and the bridges opposite the Swan public house in Moor Lane were demolished. The branch was just four years short of its centenary.

Staines West station was added to the Department of Environment's list of historic buildings in 1977 but had become derelict by this time. It was later sold by BR to Spelthorne Borough Council for the princely sum of £1. In just 37 weeks from July 1981 to April 1982 contractors converted the station into prestige offices, but

Below: A serious accident occurred at Staines Central on 9 August 1957 when an 'up' electric train passed a signal at danger and collided with a steam locomotive which had been shunting in the yard.
D. Sutton collection/Ian Allan Library

Transport Time/Price Comparisons

By road

1658 Stage coach London to Exeter via Staines 40s. (£2.00) The journey took four days. There were cheaper and less comfortable ways of travelling.
The fastest coaches took 17 hours (later 14 hours) and cost £4 5s for the single journey including tips.

1851 Omnibuses to London
Stop at the Angel & Crown, Staines. Daily there were three: one from Englefield Green, one from Sunninghill and one from Staines.
Carrier to Farringdon Market on two days per week.

1982 Green Line bus Staines to Victoria, single £1.20.

By river

1828 2/6 (12½p) per person to be rowed up from London Bridge to Staines.

1851 Barges to Upper Thames Street, London: two three times weekly, one twice weekly.

1916 Steamer: Staines to Old Windsor 8d (3p) distance c8½ miles.
Kingston to Staines 1/10 (9p) distance 15 miles.

1982 Steamer: Staines to Windsor £2.00 (no service to Kingston).

By rail

1912 Railway facilities. Both the GW & SW Companies issue cheap tickets, the return fare from Paddington or Waterloo being 2s (10p) and the weekend ticket, Friday, Saturday or Sunday, to return on Sunday, Monday or Tuesday being 2/3 (11p). There are also, of course, golfers' and anglers' tickets issued at special rates . . . 30 trains daily each way, several taking only 30 minutes to Waterloo.[15]

1938 Cheap day return Staines to Waterloo 2/2d (11p).

1982 Singe fare to Waterloo £1.70, return £3.40.

much of the structure was beyond repair and all but the main brick shell is now a replica with many detail changes. The lamp posts in the car park were originally columns which supported the platform canopy.

The Southern station, now simply known as Staines, was much rebuilt during the 1930s but has been little altered since, save for the loss of its porch some years ago. There is no freight service now, but the ancient timber goods shed still stands. The west curve, which enabled trains to run from the Reading lines to Windsor without reversal in the station, was little used and has now completely disappeared. It was on the site of the present South Street car park.

Other vanished lines in the area include the complex of sidings within the former lino works, and the Metropolitan Water Board Railway. The lino works had siding connections to both the GWR and SR lines. The former crossed the Wyrardisbury River near Staines West and is still visible as a rail across the footpath to Stanwell Moor adjacent to the Central Trading Estate. Several relics of the SR connection are visible at the back of the Central Trading Estate, including bridges alongside and under the SR lines, and the 'Lino Coal sidings' set in concrete beside the 'up' SR line adjacent to the Moormede estate. The MWB line diverged from the SR near the cattle bridge and followed the line of the present reservoir intake. A disused bridge still stands adjacent to Moormede.

Below: Small privately owned steam launch. *N. Smithers*

Staines' Inns

Staines, like many other towns, boasted a wealth of inns, drinking houses and hotels many of which have disappeared. They catered not only for the local and surrounding population but also for the numerous travellers who passed through the town. Some stopped a night or two to break their journey. Because of its position on the main road to the west and to Windsor the names of the famous who passed through the ages are too numerous to mention. Of those who stayed a night or more Nelson and Emma Hamilton, staying at the Bush, come most readily to mind.

Inn signs often tell the history of the building and its connections with the owner of the land on which it stood, eg the Angel in the High Street is on land originally the property of the Church, in this case the Abbot and Convent of St Peter, Westminster. There was an Angel inn on this site as early as 1309 and it later became a coaching inn. It was much restored and altered in 1977 but through the coaching arch can be seen remnants of early buildings.

The Blue Anchor in the Market Square, notable perhaps as our best restored and preserved old inn, has the same ecclesiastical origin. Dating back to the end of the 15th century, the upper front was rebuilt in 1700 and has many internal features of that period. The five painted curtained windows in the upper storey recall the days when this was a common avoidance of the Window Tax (abolished 1851). The lower front and bars were altered in 1904 and the adjoining shop was incorporated into the licensed house in 1915.

The White Lion on the south side of the High Street near the railway bridge was a fine half-timbered Elizabethan building. A room at the rear,

Above: The Angel & Crown. Jeweller S. H. Emary's clock, a well known landmark, has now gone. This photograph shows the site of part of Debenham's and Wayne's china shop (left centre) site of part of Johnson & Clark. *Middlesex Chronicle*

Left: The Blue Anchor and High Street c1912. *Middlesex Chronicle*

Left: The White Lion, High Street c1900. *Hist Soc collection*

Below left: The Garibaldi, High Street c1926. *Middlesex Chronicle*

Bottom: The Packhorse from the river in the 1920s. *Author's collection*

Right: The Market Square c1820. The old Market Hall where Sir Walter Raleigh was charged with high treason is at left. The Bush Inn is next to the bridge on the right; from a painting by an unknown artist. *By kind permission of the GLC Records Office*

Below right: The Bridge House Hotel from the river c1900. *Middlesex Chronicle*

the oldest part, was used from time to time as a Court Room for the local Petty Sessions, and a room with an iron grille was reputedly the lock-up. In spite of being listed for preservation the inn was demolished in 1956.

The Garibaldi on the opposite side of the High Street and just through the railway bridge, is an old building renovated in recent times. Its name is probably no earlier than the 19th century. The adjoining shop has a 16th century gable at the rear and there is a well inside the rear of the cottage next to the shop.

The Greyhound in London Road is recorded as two cottages[16] in 1859, but on another site in 1850.

The Crooked Billet has connections with the Roger Belet family and was rebuilt early in the late 19th century on a site slightly east of the original. The earliest records of the property are dated 1792.

The Three Tuns was an inn before 1674.

The Packhorse in Thames Street was probably called the Woolpack from the wool trade that passed through Staines in early times. Its licence record can be traced to the 17th century but an inn must have been on that site considerably earlier. The present main building is only about a century old. This was a favourite stopping place for boating people from the 1900s onwards. The tented roof suspended from a flagpole and extending over most of the terrace leading down to the water's edge made a very pleasant place to have tea in fine weather.

From very early times beer has been brewed in Britain and at first drinking houses brewed their own beer. The Romans hung vine leaves outside their inns and taverns, but in Britain a bush or small

make way for the approaches of the present Staines Bridge (1832). These included the creation of Clarence Street and Bridge Street.[17] The Bush name continued for a few years as the Bush and Clarence with premises extending from Clarence Street through to Church Street. The remaining half is now solely in Church Street and known as The Clarence.

The only other licensed house in Clarence Street was the Bridge House Hotel. Originally a private house of the same name it was built soon after 1832 on land surplus to the requirements of the Bridge Commissioners by Randolph Horne who was Clerk to the Commissioners. He bought the land with other plots on 6 July 1832 for £645. He founded the firm of solicitors of Horne Engall & Freeman and was Clerk to the Staines Board. After his death in 1851 his son R. H. Horne lived there.

branch showed customers when the beer was ready for drinking.

Staines had a Bush Inn in the Market Square probably from very early times. In the picture its pillared front facing the Market Square and close to the old bridge commanded an important trading position. Its extensive grounds with adequate stabling for the coaching trade extended as far as the present bridge and across Clarence Street and also included a field at the top of Bridge Street where there is now a car park. The inn was demolished as was also the Red Lion nearby to

Later occupants were Arthur Finch (about 1880) who, with his brother Charles owned the Mustard Mill, two Miss Finches and a Miss Fletcher. Thomas William Taylor ('Tom Taylor') bought the house about 1898 and turned it into a hotel. He built on a red brick extension designed by Ralph Lowe a local architect in place of greenhouses on the Colne side. As a hotel it was unusual in several ways: it had two main staircases; on the bridge side it had 20 single bedrooms for London commuters; it was the first house to have its own electricity in Staines; it had a fine mulberry tree on the shady terraced lawn

Top: The North Star, Kingston Road, in 1980. *Chris Leigh*

Centre: The Bells, Thames Street/Binbury Row in 1979.
Staines & Egham News

Above: The Swan, Moor Lane in 1974.
Middlesex Chronicle

Vanished Inns and Drinking Houses

In the High Street
The Cabin. Ceased to trade in 1957, demolished a few years later.
The Crown and Anchor. Demolished 1957.
The White Lion (sometimes known as the White Horse). Demolished 1956.
The White Swan (had disappeared by 1824) had been described as 'near The Middle Rowe' which was a group of houses in the middle of the High Streer near Thames Street which were demolished in 1802. Nearby was the Green Dragon (recorded in 16th century).

Market Square
The Bush Inn and Posting House.
The Bush Tap (which may have been The Running Horse) with a separate tenancy; and the Red Lion Inn were all cleared away for the building of the 1832 bridge and the creation of its access road, Clarence Street.
The Mail Coach Beer House (on the south side of the square).
The Black Boy (on the corner of Blackboy Lane).
The Kings Head (by 1871 a tramps' lodging house). These three with the lane were swept away for the building of the new Town Hall 1879/80. The Memorial Gardens now occupy part of the site of Blackboy Lane.

Church Street
The Waterman's Arms (ceased trading c1904); The George Inn, junction with High Street (recorded in the 15th century, ceased trading in the 18th and demolished in the 19th).

Kingston Road
The Turk's Head near George Street (recorded 1869).

London Road
The Hope, corner of New Street.
The Wagon and Horses closed about 1912.
The New Inn, opposite Shortwood Avenue, by a tollgate on the Bedfont to Bagshot Turnpike.
The Horse and Groom to be found on a map of c1800.

Sites Unknown
The Bear and The Dog where both had some troops billetted about 1690.
The Castle, The Crispin, The Nag's Head, and The Rose and Crown — all licenced in 1730 and may appear under another name in this list.

leading down to the river; and it had a licence for dancing for one side of the hotel as distinct from the licensed premises on the other. The only other licence for dancing at that time was held by the Railway Hotel. Tom Taylor had a boatyard between the Hotel and the bridge with a slipway for houseboats and steamers which his firm built there. For storage he leased some of the arches under Staines bridge. In 1901 his firm, Tom Taylor & Sons acquired land and built works on the Surrey side of the river which are still in existence. The hotel was sold to a Mrs Marshall in 1922 and was taken over by the Official Receiver in 1929 but continued as a hotel. It was pulled down about 1935.[18] The Regal Cinema (later known as the ABC Cinema) opened on the site in 1939. In recent years it was much altered internally and now has three cinemas under one roof. The site of Taylor's Bridge House boatyard is now occupied by the new Bridge Hotel. (Built 1973/4 and altered 1980.)

The Railway Hotel (now known as the Gay Cavalier) owes its origin to the coming of the London & South Western Railway to Staines in 1848. The North Star, called after a famous GWR British single driver 2-2-2 engine of 1837 is still in Kingston Road, its front elevation unaltered today. Before the days of the Railways is the Old Red Lion near the smithy in Leacroft and Jolly Butcher by the tollgate on the turnpike road to Sunbury. Further down the road is the Dog and Partridge (1958) whose licence was transferred from another similarly named whose site at Hatton was taken over by London Airport. Reflecting the rural area

Top: The White Lion which stood at the point where South Street now joins High Street.
B. Ashworth collection

Above:The Blue Anchor frontage in 1980 after the structure had been damaged when an arsonist destroyed the adjacent shops. Note the false windows and the much earlier timber-framed structure which adjoins the rear of the hotel. *Chris Leigh*

Left: This 1980 view of the Angel Hotel makes an interesting comparison with earlier views. In 1976 the DoE refused to add the hotel to its list of protected buildings because it had undergone so many alterations. The actual building pre-dates both its 'genuine' Georgian frontage visible in early photographs, and the present 20th century-built 'Elizabethan' facade. *Chris Leigh*

are The Beehive and The Wheatsheaf and Pigeon off the Laleham Road.

The Great Western Railway came to Staines in 1884/5 in opposition to the LSW Railway, but there was no need for a new inn nearby as, less than 100 yards away, Church Street had four inns. The Phoenix is known to have been licensed in 1730 but there was probably an earlier building

and today's building may be early 19th century. The Cock is recorded in the 15th century. It is highly probable that the present building dates from 1832 when Bridge Street was created at the time when the 1832 bridge was built. The Bells originally called the Bell because of its proximity to St Mary's church. It was an inn of some importance in Stuart times. The Waterman's Arms (south side of Church Street),[19] catering mainly no doubt for the bargemen when there was considerable barge traffic on the short cut between the Lammas and St Mary's church known as Bargeman's Creek which went to Poyle paper mills. It probably attracted main stream barge traffic particularly bargemen from barges that tied up at the wharf by Binbury Row as did the barges carrying stone for the repair of the Round Tower at Windsor. Closure came soon after the canal ceased about 1904.

Over in Moor Lane and seemingly divorced from the rest of Staines is The Swan which catered for the small community there and also, no doubt, for parishioners who had the right to graze horses and cattle on the nearby common land.

Staines' High Street

The major change to the High Street in recent times has been the creation of the Elmsleigh shopping centre which necessitated the demolition of a number of buildings, notably the old premises of Mumford & Lobb's furniture shop and warehouse. Behind the High Street the clearance of buildings included Elmsleigh House. Built about 1878 this house was owned for some time by the Ashby family. Residents included the Doctors Tothill from c1880 to 1916 and Dr Henry Bergh. In 1952 the Staines Urban District Council used Elmsleigh House for its clerk's department until shortly before it was demolished in 1974. Other changes behind the High Street included the clearance of the Quaker burial ground and meeting hut; the removal of the synagogue to a new site; in Thames Street the demolition of shops, the old Margaret Pope School and the Bowling Club with its beautifully kept green; and the complete disappearance of Tothill Street.

Elmsleigh shopping centre was opened by Her

Right: Junction of High Street and Church Street 1980. The shop on the corner is Victorian and those on the right in Church Street are Cromwellian.
Chris Leigh

Below: Junction of High Street and Church Street c1820. The old George Inn is in the foreground; from an oil painting, artist unknown.
By permission of the GLC Record Office

Majesty Queen Elizabeth II on Friday 22 February 1980. She was accompanied by Prince Philip. At the High Street entrance she was welcomed by the Mayor of Spelthorne, Geoff Kaye, the Lord Lieutenant of Surrey, Lord Hamilton of Dalzell, and Mr Humphrey Atkins, MP for Spelthorne and the then Secretary of State for Northern Ireland. South Street has been made to link the Centre to the High Street and Thames Street. The completion on the north side in 1981/2 by Spelthorne Borough Council includes a large County library, Citizens' Advice Bureau, a small office suite, a car park and six large shopping units with a pedestrian mall leading from the bus station to the shops and library. On the southern part of the site a group of companies are opening an office block of similar design and brickwork to the Elmsleigh Centre.

Top left: The modern High Street with the new telephone exchange in the centre background. *Staines & Egham News*

Top right: Victorian Cottages, George Street (off Kingston Road). *Tony Keen*

Above: The Victorian High Street c1880/1890. *Hist Soc collection*

Right: The old High Street with the White Lion in the centre background. *Middlesex Chronicle*

Left: Decorations in the High Street in 1902 to celebrate the end of the Boer War. *Hist Soc collection*

Below: Decorations in the High Street on 12 May 1937 to celebrate the coronation of King George VI. *Middlesex Chronicle*

Bottom: The High Street looking towards the Police station with the now demolished Majestic cinema on the left and beyond it, the Post Office. *B. Ashworth collection*

Below: The old post office, High Street. J. Little, postmaster 1886–91, is in straw hat. *Hist Soc collection*

Below right: HM Queen Elizabeth II at the opening of the Elmsleigh Shopping Centre, Staines on 22 February 1980. *Middlesex Chronicle*

Above: The new post office built 1931; the Majestic cinema, built 1929 and demolished 1961, was on site of 'Fairfield' where lived Dr de la Motte. It later became a nunnery and then a hotel 'Marmaduke's', later renamed 'VIIs'. *Middlesex Chronicle*

Above: The High Street with Norris Road visible on the left. In the centre distance is the White Lion, and beyond it the original low wrought iron railway bridge.   *B. Ashworth collection*

Left: Rowe & Sons, builders; the shop also sold wallpaper and ironmongery. The photograph is dated 1869.
Tony Keen from an original

Below: The Trustee Savings Bank, Kingston Road in the same, restored, building. A 1975 view. This building together with some shops in Kingston Road and some houses in George Street round the corner off Kingston Road are to be demolished to make way for development. Application has already been made to Spelthorne Borough Council for Planning Permission and it seems certain it will be granted. The application was published in the *Staines & Egham News,* Spelthorne Edition, Issue of 22 May 1981.   *Tony Keen*

Spelthorne Borough Council and Staines Emergency Services

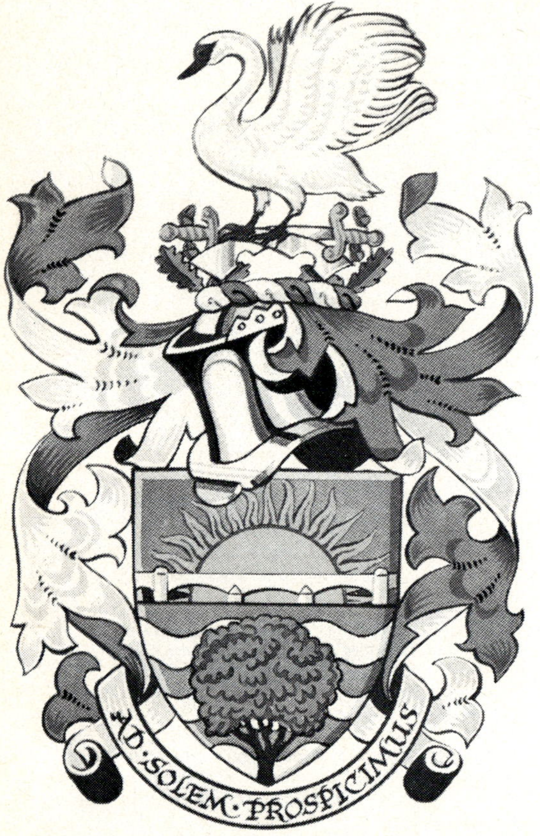

Above: The Borough of Spelthorne coat of arms, 1974.
By permission of the Borough of Spelthorne

Below left: The Parish Council Coat of Arms (not under patent) on the Town Hall.
By permission of the Borough of Spelthorne

Below right: The Staines UDC coat of arms (Grant of Arms 19 July 1951).
By permission of the Borough of Spelthorne

Above: The Town Hall, Market Square, was built in 1880 and designed by John Johnson of Mansion House, London. The clock was made by Gillett & Johnson of Croydon and has three faces, the one above the market square having two XIs for the hours 9 and 11. The Court for Sunbury & Staines Sessions was held in the Town Hall from October 1967 to March 1976. *Chris Leigh*

Below: Detail of the upper part of the front of the Town Hall showing the parish council 'coat of arms' which had no Patent. *Chris Leigh*

DEMAND NOTE.

PARISH AND URBAN DISTRICT OF STAINES.
(STAINES UNION).

Mr. *W. S. Biffen*

The Overseers of the Poor demand payment of **A POOR RATE** made the 3rd day of April, 1916, to meet expenses which will be incurred during the half-year ending the 30th day of September, 1916, **now due from you**, in respect of the Hereditaments of which the Assessment Number and the Rateable value are stated below:

Assessment Number.	Description of Property	Rateable Value.	Amount of Rate at 1s. in the £ on Agricultural Land and 2s. in the £ on other Hereditaments.		
		£	£	s.	d.
1897	Buildings and other Hereditaments not being Agricultural Land	28	2	16	-
	Agricultural Land				
	TOTAL.... £				

Amount payable by Owner, provided it be paid within the time prescribed by Section 5 of the Poor Rate Assessment and Collection Act, 1869. £

The Urban District Council of Staines demands payment of the undermentioned Rate made the 3rd day of April, 1916, for expenses incurred or to be incurred during the half-year ending the 30th day of September, 1916, **now due from you :—**

General District Rate at 2s. 4d. in the £

On full rateable value of property other than Land etc. 1 7 4

On one-fourth rateable value of Land etc. ... ...

On 70 per cent. of rateable value of Cottages (where Owner is assessed)

NOTE. SEWERAGE PORTION £ 1 8 IS DEDUCTED FROM THE GENERAL DISTRICT RATE.

Total Amount of Rates demanded ... ... £ 4 13 4

Purposes for which the above-mentioned Poor Rate was made and amount in the £ levied for each purpose, half the amount being levied on Agricultural Land:—		THE GENERAL DISTRICT RATE is made to meet the estimated expenses for the half-year ending 30th September, 1916, and includes the cost of:
Amount in the Pound	s. d.	Sewerage, Repairs of Highways, Main and other Roads (including Scavenging) Collection and Disposal of House Refuse, Watering, Lighting, Street Works and Improvements, Pleasure Grounds, Mortuary, Nuisances Abatement, Fire Brigade, Hospital, Allotments, Salaries, Other Establishment Charges, Legal Expenses, Repayment of Loans with interest, &c.
Relief of the Poor and other Expenses of the Guardians	0 5	
County Contributions (Including Education Expenses)	1 3	F. C. HOARE,
Police Rate	0 4	*Assistant Overseer and Collector*
TOTAL	2 0	CONISTON, GREENLANDS ROAD, STAINES.

Cheques should be made payable to the above-named Collector and crossed "BARCLAY & Co. ......" The Collector attends at the TOWN HALL every WEDNESDAY ...... o'clock, to receive the Rates. *Please forward this Demand Note* ......

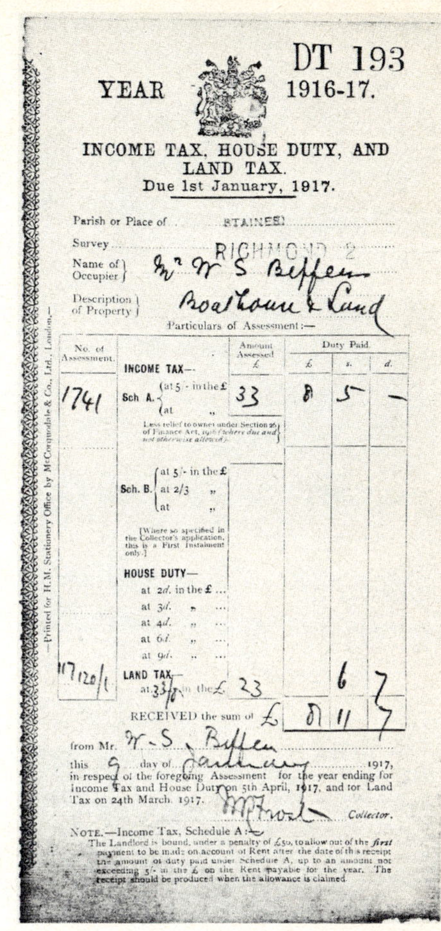

YEAR 1916-17. DT 193

INCOME TAX, HOUSE DUTY, AND LAND TAX.
Due 1st January, 1917.

Parish or Place of ...... STAINES

Survey ...... RICHMOND 2

Name of Occupier } *Mr W. S. Biffen*

Description of Property } *Boat House & Land*

Particulars of Assessment :—

No. of Assessment.		Amount Assessed £	Duty Paid.		
			£	s.	d.
1741	**INCOME TAX—** Sch. A. (at 5/- in the £ (at	33	8	5	-
	Less relief to owner under Section 25 of Finance Act, 1916 (where due and not otherwise allowed).				
	Sch. B. (at 5/- in the £ (at 2/3 (at				
	[Where so specified in the Collector's application, this is a First Instalment only.]				
	HOUSE DUTY— at 2d. in the £ ... at 3d. ,, ,, at 4d. ,, ,, at 6d. ,, ,, at 9d. ,, ,,				
17/20/1	**LAND TAX—** at 3⅜d. in the £	23		6	7

RECEIVED the sum of £ ... 8 11 ...

from Mr. *W. S. Biffen*

this *9* day of *January* ...... 1917, in respect of the foregoing Assessment for the year ending for Income Tax and House Duty on 5th April, 1917, and for Land Tax on 24th March, 1917.

...... *Collector.*

NOTE.—Income Tax, Schedule A :— The Landlord is bound, under a penalty of £50, to allow out of the *first* payment to be made on account of Rent after the date of this receipt the amount of duty paid under Schedule A, up to an amount not exceeding 5/- in the £ on the Rent payable for the year. This receipt should be produced when the allowance is claimed.

Printed for H.M. Stationery Office by McCorquodale & Co., Ltd., London.

Above left: Staines Urban District Rates Demand for 1916. The General District Rate was 2s 4d (12p) in the pound. (The Spelthorne Borough Council 1979/80 General Rate was £1 17p in the pound.)

Above: Income Tax and Land Tax Demand for 1916/17: Schedule A 5/- (25p) in the pound: Land Tax $3\frac{3}{8}$d (1½p) in the pound. (Standard rate of Income Tax in 1980 30p in the pound.)

Left: The Civic Centre, Kingston Road, was opened in September 1972. The Spelthorne Borough Council coat of arms is displayed above the main entrance.
Tony Keen

Staines Police Staion

It is known that in 1864 Staines was policed by the Metropolitan Police, the area being governed by senior officers from Kensington. The exact site of the police station at that time is not known with certainty, but is believed to have been the old Bow Street Runners' station which had a captain, a corporal and five troopers or townsmen. This was in London Road at the junction with Swinburn Lane which led to Stanwell Moor.[20] The three roads, to

London, to Kingston, and Staines High Street could be watched from this station and farm cart and other traffic could be controlled to keep the way clear for the frequent passage of regular mail coaches and other coaches through Staines. The building later became the Orange Cafe whose proprietor used one cell as a cool room. It was still in perfect order when most of the building was demolished to make way for offices. What remains today is No 1 London Road beside Staines House.

About 1865 the police moved to Dearle's Meadow in Kingston Road (later the site of the candle factory). The site proved unsatisfactory and another, Nightingale's Field, reputedly priced at £500 was chosen. At the end of September 1875 a temporary building (on the site now occupied by Kingston Road School) was occupied until the new building was completed in June 1876, with partial occupation in April. A certain amount of mystery surrounds the building of the police station. A single storey building on the site had been used as a doctor's practice and poor people's dispensary by a former major of the Indian medical service and late of the Honourable East India Company. It is believed that for police use an extra storey was built on to this. Looking at the building it can be seen that the bricks above the lower window arches are of a slightly different colour. This is more noticeable when they are wet after heavy rain. The lower bricks are of a harder, local type and the lower window arches are of an earlier design than the upper arches.

In the 1880s a bricklayer, 'Socky' Bolton, who lived in Swinburn Lane, built or rebuilt the cells. Interestingly, an occurrence book was found under the floorboards of the police station in 1968 and adds a bit more information about 'Socky' Bolton. On completion of his work he went to the White Horse Inn (sometimes known as the White Lion) to celebrate and was later arrested for being drunk and disorderly and became the first inmate of the cells which he had built. The next day he had to walk beside a mounted policeman to Bedfont Petty Sessions where he was fined 1/- (5p) with a further 1/- costs. From the court he had to walk to Bedfont police station to collect his possessions and from there back to Staines. No doubt he walked off his hangover.

Above: Benjamin Rosenthal served in the 12th Lancers for five years and left the army in December 1875, joining the Metropolitan Police in January 1876. He was transferred to the mounted branch and from there to Staines in 1890 (then aged 50), where he was one of the first three mounted police and retired in 1895. During World War 1 he changed his name to Ralph (his eldest son's name). His reason for this was that another Rosenthal of German origin betrayed British secrets to Germany and was executed as a spy. PC Ralph died when he was within a few days of his 80th birthday. His son served in the South Wales Borderers, later joined the Surrey Police and is buried in Laleham churchyard.
J. Livermore collection

Right: Regular Police from Staines who lined the route in London for the coronation of King George V in 1910.
J. Livermore collection

In later years stables for three horses were built for the station with a flat above for a married officer. Later this building became a canteen. The station itself was given a facelift in 1970 and in 1978/9 major construction alterations were made so that it is now a first class up-to-date unit.

The Staines Fire Brigade

The most treasured relic of Staines Fire Brigade is the old manual engine of 1738. Restored in 1979, it is now exhibited in the Staines Museum which, appropriately, is in the old fire station by the Town Hall. The 1738 engine hoses were made of leather as also were the firemen's helmets. There was probably an earlier engine. An Act of 1832 laid down the equipment to be used, but no provision was made for the payment of members. The first brigade was therefore composed of volunteers, each member bought his own uniform and there was a waiting list of 12.[21] By 1893 there seems to have been an improvement since rule 12 of 1st January 1893 states, 'That all fires Members shall be paid 1/- (5p) per hour for the time they are at the fire and time spent in reaching and returning from fire. Three hours extra shall be given per man for cleaning Engine and gear, but any Member absent from cleaning shall forfeit his 3/- (15p) which shall be put into the Fire Brigade Fund'.

In 1800 a new manual engine was acquired, in 1876 a Merryweather 'steamer', in 1924 a Dennis, and in 1935 a Leyland.

The Brigade Diary gives the following interesting, and in some cases hair raising, information:

November 1887, the brigade was called out by a man on a tricycle, and by telegram in 1896!

Its duties, in addition to fire fighting, included firing a royal salute from the top of the Town Hall, joining the parade to celebrate the relief of Mafeking, and making up part of the Guard of Honour for Queen Victoria's funeral at Windsor. In May 1896 it assisted Richmond Brigade, but area co-operation fell into disuse until World War 2.[22]

The brigade's headquarters were moved to the present Fire Station in Town Lane, Stanwell in

Right: Old Staines Fire Station, Market Square (now the Museum). *Middlesex Chronicle*

Below: Staines town old fire engine of 1738. *Staines & Egham News*

Bottom: Steam fire engine and crew 1880, Staines Linoleum Manufacturing Company. *Hist Soc collection*

1963. Its modern equipment is designed to cope with today's variety of fires, including electrical and chemical fires, and it has equipment for freeing victims trapped in car accidents. It has an average incident turnout of 85-100 a month.

A local resident, Mrs Elsie Cleary, has an interesting connection with the history of the Metropolitan Fire Brigade. Her father, Ernest Robert Protheroe, drove the first Merryweather motor fire engine for the London fire brigade in 1904. He was stationed mainly at the headquarters of the brigade as Sub Officer at Southwark Bridge Road. The proud possessor of their No 1 driving licence, he became driving instructor for the London Fire Brigade.[23]

Staines during World War 2

Ask anyone who was in Staines how the war affected them and most will reply that they cannot remember much and they don't think the town was much affected by the war. Perhaps this is because London, so near, suffered heavily, Staines by comparison much less. Yet it had its share of bombing, destruction of homes and its tragedies.

Between 1939 and 1940 incendiary bombs were dropped on the town itself in Hale Street and Rosefield Road and phosphorous, high explosive and incendiaries on various points between Laleham Road and the Wheatsheaf Lane area, in Pavilion Gardens, and from George Street across to Gresham and Edgell Roads. A stick of 11 HE (two unexploded) straddled the George VI reservoir which although recently completed had not been filled with water. A mock-up of Clapham Junction had been made inside it and this must have fooled the enemy bombers. This decoy was activated on the night of the biggest raid on 23 February 1944 when 10,000 incendiaries were dropped. Most fell on soft ground on Staines Moor doing little damage there, but the GWR line was cut nearby and Viola

Avenue in Stanwell suffered heavily. Also inside the reservoir was a meteorological office which was hit by a flying bomb in the same year killing the met officer who manned it. The nearby twin reservoirs were also bombed but to a lesser degree. Flying bombs in 1944 were dropped on Staines Moor near Spout Lane, between Horton Road and the river Colne near Moor Lane and on the Wraysbury Road near The Lammas. Ashford also suffered heavily. The worst fatalities in Staines were in Stainash Crescent where there were four killed and 17 injured.

At one period, to combat enemy planes, a nightly train ran up and down the stretch of Southern railway line which runs parallel with the Causeway. Mounted on trucks were some very noisy ack ack guns. Perhaps these were mobile 45s. Lord 'Germany calling' Haw Haw bombed the area (in words only) twice, saying that Bell Weir

Below: ARP gas van 18–23 July 1938 on site of present Bridge Street car park. *Hist Soc collection*

had been destroyed and that St Mary's church clock had been stopped. Neither news item was true.

Staines soon had its LDV (Local Defence Volunteers), later called the Home Guard, in training. 'Dad's Army' is too close to the truth for comfort at least at the beginning. We can enjoy it on television now but then it was hardly hilarious when boathooks, which some referred to as pikes, were issued as an item of their equipment (for defence?!). Later wooden rifles specially weighted to feel like the real thing were issued so that they could practice rifle drill. A kind of wild do-it-yourself optimism was in the air. Two residents of Rosefield Road were going on fire watching duty one night. One asked his companion, 'what's that bulging under your jacket Bill?' The other drew out a large axe 'This', he said, 'and if any of those Germans come down here I'll chop his bloody head off.'

The ambulance service part of the ARP organisation had women drivers at first. It began, as everything else, without badge or uniform. For a time they wore home-made armbands. One of the drivers went on duty in her ski suit and was probably the most comfortably dressed of them all. Ambulances were commandeered by the local Council, one was an ancient butcher's van with parts of the body tied up with string, another a

Above: War Weapons Week, May 1941.
Hist Soc collection

Below: A view of bomb damage to Stainash Crescent, 1944. *Dennis Sutton*

Right: VJ-Day street party in the Richmond Road.

Below right: Quaker hut canteen for the wounded, December 1944. *Evening News*

furniture pantechnicon which, when empty,
swayed alarmingly in a slight wind or at any speed
over 20mph. It had no noticeable brakes and some
gear changing skill with good timing was necessary
to bring it to a halt at the right spot. Staines was no
different from anywhere else in those early days.
Later of course things improved. The Auxiliary Fire
Service, stationed in London Road, Ashford, was
equipped throughout the war with six civilian cars
and two lorries with ladders perched on top. In
spite of this amazing equipment its members did
valiant service. The Civil Defence Control Centre
was in the Town Hall and later moved to the former
Engineer's department of the Staines UDC in
Shortwood House, London Road, the Town Hall
becoming the reserve centre.

Local Councils were responsible for many
services: ambulances, food distribution and the
issue of ration cards, ARP, fire watching, etc. The
Lord of the Manor, Harry Scott Freeman, who also
happened to be clerk to the Staines UDC, was Food
Officer for the district with responsibility to the
Ministry of Food and was also Controller of the
local ARP organisation. Chairman of the local Food
Control Committee for ten years was Herbert W.
Green, a former Council chairman three times,
secretary to the moormasters and connected with
many local organisations. He was works cashier at
Staines Lino and much loved and respected.

Among various special war industries in the
town were Hoover who took over the upper part of
Perrings furniture premises working as sub-
contractors making wiring for Lancasters and
Halifaxes; Lagonda cars, just over the border in
Egham made munitions and had an alarm control
post for all factories in the area who continued
work during an alert until bombers or flying bombs
were sighted 10 miles away.

Torpedoes were made at the Staines linoleum
works which was taken over for the duration by the
navy. The WRNS were quartered at Moor House. A
firm in the High Street made sten guns at 7/9d
(39p) a time, and F. Lewis, house furnishers in the
High Street made baskets for medical supplies to
be parachuted into Arnhem. Some residents were
directed to war work outside the area, eg to Bates'
boatyard at Chertsey where MTBs and fire tenders

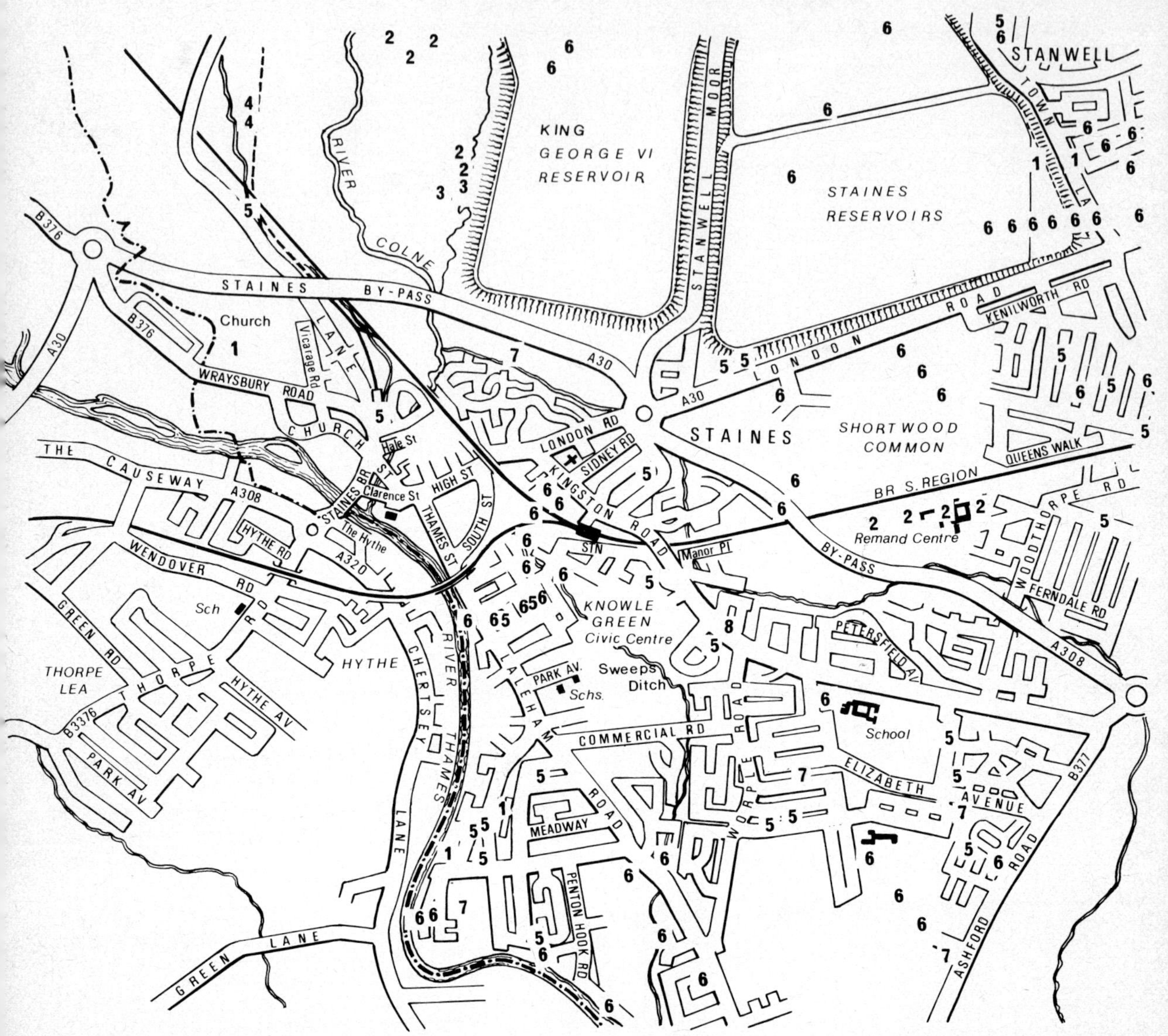

Raid of 23-2-44

1 Phosphorus Bombs

2 High Explosive

3 High Explosive (unexploded)

4 Incendiary Bombs Containers

September 1939 to January 1940

5 Incendiary Bombs

6 High Explosive

7 High Explosive (unexploded)

8 Flying Bomb (19-6-44)

Note: Locations imposed on up-to-date map

were built and where also many old boats were made seaworthy for the trip to Dunkirk. The twin Staines reservoirs were used by the RAF as a practice area in 1943 for dropping the bouncing bombs used against the Mohne Dam which was bombed on the same night as the Sorpe and Eder dams. Local residents were mystified by the RAF activity over the reservoirs as the high banks which surrounded them hid the water surface from their view. Shortwood Common became a tank testing ground.

Some visible signs of early war preparations were part of a national plan. In 1940 concrete lined sockets were inserted across the roadway of Staines bridge. These were filled with wooden plugs which could be removed for the insertion of steel tank trap posts; the ground floor of the Literary & Scientific Institute but recently an antique furniture gallery, became a reinforced strong point commanding the bridge though it is doubtful if anti-tank guns were available for it then; and down the Thames, anchored midstream at intervals, were barges to prevent hostile seaplanes from landing, and the river was patrolled nightly by motor boat. The temporary bridge was built over the Thames near the bridge in 1941 presumably to take some of the burden of military traffic away from the road bridge. Later the allied leaders were

to meet at Stanwell Place to make their plans for D-Day. All sections of the ARP (Home Defence) organisation played an important part in dealing with the effect of air raids when sleepless nights were the norm and humanity and efficiency went hand in hand.

Mr A. O. Mitchell, in his capacity as Deputy Surveyor to the Council, had to do duty at Wimbledon Town Hall where there were spotters on the roof and an ops room in the basement. While he was away, sometimes for several days, his wife and young daughter were alone in their home on the Causeway, taking cover whenever necessary, and always at night, in an indoor shelter. She had company, however, night after night. In her garden Canadian troops (in peacetime lumber jacks) elected to sleep off their visit to Staines before returning to their camp in Egham before reveillé. They used to call to her through the letter box to cheer her up!

There were some wonderful voluntary services, eg the WVS under the leadership of Mrs Bergh had a canteen in the High Street. In the Quaker hut behind the High Street Mrs Lewis with the aid of willing and hard working members of the Staines Evening Townswomen's Guild ran a free canteen for the wounded from hospitals including Ashford Hospital, St Peter's in Chertsey and a military hospital in Ascot. Started in June 1940 it carried on until October 1945. Contributions from the Guild and a weekly voucher for bread from the Staines Rotarians were used to purchase food. The visitors' books bear witness to the smiling faces of the hostesses and their homely welcome to the troops. There are signatures of men from all branches of the services and of foreign, American and Dominions troops. The remarks written vary from 'we came, we saw, we were conquered' in latin and 'we heard of this place in the desert' to 'new bread! We did not think there was any such thing' and 'Tea! with SUGAR!'

A mutual friendship hour was run by another group of citizens to cheer up old people and others who had lost their homes and everything they owned in the blitz, many of whom had been evacuated from London.

This then was Staines during the war. There must be many more stories untold. People are inclined to be reticent. It is history now and perhaps those who went through it just want to forget — and who could blame them?

Boys' Schools in Staines

Compiled from Log Books of the National School 1863–93 and the British School 1867–1903 by S. F. Cotton BA

Staines' boys' schools had existed prior to 1863. The British and Foreign School Society was founded in 1808 and the National School Society in 1811. The British Schools catered for Non-conformists and Quakers, and the National School for those who attended Church of England Sunday School and whose parents went to church. Attendance at church from school was made on Ascension Day, Ash Wednesday and during Holy week, and the Vicar took a weekly class. The fees, a few coppers per week, were paid by the parents, or by wealthy ladies or employers or, in the case of orphans, by the Guardians. The charge for those who lived outside the parish of Staines was double, but on occasion, due to overcrowding, outsiders were refused. There was a certain amount of competition between the schools and transfers were occasionally made, but not if fees were outstanding. Boys were reported to have left the British School because 'the work was too hard', 'the children were taught too much', 'they did not need fractions' or 'geography', one of the additional subjects sometimes taught over and above the 'three Rs'.

The National School had been in Thames Street but moved in 1864 to St Mary's Hall, London Road where there was a hall 60ft by 25ft, and one classroom 25ft by 12ft. Numbers on roll vary from 79 to 185. The playground and space for drill was the London road itself! The Vicar examined the children annually and there was a prizegiving in December. There was a Master-in-Charge, probably trained at St John's Training College, Battersea, and occasionally an Assistant Master. These instructed the Pupil Teachers, boys of 14 to 18, who then taught the various classes. The Master also had Sunday and other duties in connection with the church.

The British School was held in various places, including the Society of Friends' House in Blackboy Lane, but in 1875 a new school in Thames Street was opened. The hall was 45ft by 20ft and the classroom 20ft by 14ft and the numbers varied from 41 to 155. There was some congestion at times, 10 to a desk being reported. The Ashby family usually provided the Chairman of the Managers until 1885 when the School Board took over. The Master taught the Pupil teachers, starting variously at 6.30am, 7.15am or 8–9am, in the dinner hour 1.00 till 2.00, and in the evenings. In addition he supervised the school during the mornings and afternoons, teaching those classes where he felt the need was greatest. The Pupil Teachers had homework as well, and usually went to Borough Road College (then in Southwark) at 18. In both schools the heating was by means of open fires, later replaced by stoves which were liable to smoke. The lighting was by oil lamps, which were replaced by gas in 1875. The school cleaner was paid 2/6 (12$\frac{1}{2}$p) per week, increased to 3/6 (17$\frac{1}{2}$p) in the winter when she had the fires to light and to provide the kindling wood. The playground at the British School was covered with sand in 1881, and with asphalt in 1897. The lavatories were external and frequent blockages of the drains were noted in the log. The water taps were frozen for several weeks in 1891 and water was fetched from houses nearby.

The authorities of the school were responsible for the finance, and the fees from the parents were augmented by grants from the government paid on results. HM Inspectors tested the pupils in their classes and expected boys to be up to standards

Left: The Margaret Pope British School, located in Thames Street 1874–1903, was demolished in November 1973. *Tony Keen*

Right: London Road in 1976. The gabled building on the right is St Mary's Hall. The inn right foreground is the Greyhound.
Staines & Egham News

according to their age. The amounts were small, 4/-
(20p) per subject per year for each of the three Rs,
and 3/- (15p) each for up to two extra subjects.
Occasionally the schools earned little grant and
money was usually tight. Materials, slates and
books were in short supply. Each time the
Inspectors visited the school they wrote a report
which was copied into the log. Matthew Arnold
signed the British School Log Book on several
occasions.

Since the Staines area was then largely
agricultural, the month's holiday in the summer
was called the Harvest Holiday. There was a
fortnight at Christmas, 10 days at Easter, Whit
Monday and Tuesday, a day at Staines Fair
(11 May) a half day for the Regatta. The National
School had a school treat and the British School
had a dinner followed by an outing to Hampton
Court, Kew Gardens, Runnymede or Virginia
Water.

Attendances were much affected by the
weather. Snow, floods, slippery roads, excessive
rain or heat were all quoted as reasons for a low
attendance, as were broken chilblains, smallpox
(1871), measles and fever. The hay harvest or a
late corn harvest affected attendances, and boys
were also sent gleaning. Friday afternoons and
Mondays were occasionally thin, and special
occasions such as Garlanding and May Day, the
Onion Fair (19 September), Chertsey and Stanwell
Fairs; Egham, Ascot and Chertsey Horse Races
were noted, as well as the circus and Band of Hope
outings. Various Sunday School treats affected the
British School as the boys were of various
denominations. National holidays for the Golden
and Diamond Jubilees of the Queen were recorded,
as was a day when the Queen visited Egham.

The system of payment by results meant a lot of
learning by rote. Discipline was pretty strict and
classes were kept in to learn catechisms, collects or
other lessons. A flogging is reported for truancy,
and expulsions were recorded because of
interference of the parents in school matters or
routine. In some years the poems and songs to be
learned by each class are recorded. Visual and
other aids towards interesting the boys included
the Magic Lantern, Dissolving Views, copies of
Titbits and Pearson's Weekly, educational games,
specimens of rocks sent by teachers in mining
districts, and at the break up at term end there
might be a distribution of sweets, nuts and/or
apples.

Flowers and Wildlife at the Old Nursery

J. Livermore

Before the population explosion in the Worple Road area of the 1950s and 1960s, the tract of land which lay south of the unmade road at Commercial Road extending to Worple Road was partially used as a nursery. Much of the hedgerow was sheltered by thick hawthorn bushes reaching a height of eight feet or more. In this sheltered haven, free of cats and other predators, wildlife was supreme. Garden birds and extra shy varieties met in harmony. Greenfinches, chaffinches and goldfinches chattered away oblivious of the larger thrushes and other similar birds. It was there that I saw my first waxwing in January 1957. The weather was very cold with severe gales, blizzards and foul weather in Scandinavia and most northern areas. I noticed a pair of chestnut brown birds with magnificent crests sweeping from the bridge of the beak back over the black-lined eyes. A red bar in the wings looked as bright as sealing wax. About seven inches long, the tail reminiscent of a jay, when they sat quite still they looked as if made of porcelain. Among a quarrelsome family of sparrows they seemed like giants surrounded by a group of dwarfs. Other visitors were bramblings or bramble finches their feathers as dull as hen chaffinches, but by the end of February or the beginning of March before they left, the cock had started to grow his courting feathers and was much brighter. Although the bramblings mixed with the other finches, they rarely moved more than about a hundred yards from an old beech tree.

This gnarled old tree was the first to be bulldozed away. At some time it had been blown down but still continued to live horizontal to the ground. Part of the trunk was covered by ivy with a purple flower standing on a long neck. This was a haven for some very small and active wood voles. Later, in March, large clumps of dark-leaved plants could be seen under the tree. This new year's growth not yet fully mature had long strings of minute flowers very much like the stinging nettle. This was Dog Mercury, a wind flower without petals, the longer strings bearing stamens and the shorter, petals. Nearby was a wood violet, its heart shaped, glossy leaves formed in a tight rosette. Just inside the fence was a tangled, leafless Wild Plum, later to be covered in snow white flowers. About 10 yards from the plum tree was a clump measuring about three feet by one foot of pale, sweet scented Sweet Violets with very large downy heart shaped leaves. Later when the weather improved many bees came, but were too late for the main crop of blossom.

In April some wild white anemones appeared. Unlike many flowers, the anemone does not produce nectar, so the bees visiting them got only a dusting of pollen. Thriving there also although out of its usual territory was Wood Sorrel its trefoils looking like large pale clover leaves, its single pure white blossoms on single stalks tinged with fine lines of purple to show the way to its nectar. The seed pods were at first hidden under the leaves, but just before the pods were ripe the stalk seemed to extend itself above the foliage so that the seeds could be scattered unimpeded by the foliage. The seed pods exploded with an audible crack like the breaking of a well filled pea pod.

Towards the ditch at the Commercial Road end was a Clematis which seemed to survive year after year. Climbing up the hedge the little corner was filled with its greenish white flowers in July and August and in winter it lightened the drab hedge with its lengthened pistils of feathery plumes known as Old Man's Beard. Nearby, a member of the cucumber family, the White Briony climbed like a grape vine around an old gnarled crab apple tree. Its large greenish white flowers developing in autumn into bright red berries. In harmony a great hedge bindweed pushed its large white trumpet flowers through masses of weed.

Among this wealth of plant life lived a family of hedgehogs. In the light summer mornings the young ones would roll in the grass and with the parents would slowly walk to the ditch which always had water for them to drink. By the stream I took a bird count. Marking out a three yard square which included a small tree and a thick bush I scattered bird seed suitable for a variety of birds. In half an hour I counted 38 chaffinch, five robin, two willow warblers, five wren, seven pied wagtail, 11 blue tit, two great tit, four coal tit, two gold crest, five missel thrush, nine song thrush, seven blackbirds, four linnets, 13 goldfinch, 17 greenfinch, eight starling, one bramblefinch, one tree sparrow, 21 sparrows, a green woodpecker, a magpie, a pair of jays and what at first I thought was a bird escaped from an aviary, but was in fact a golden oriole. I also caught a glimpse of what I thought was an owl, but it was gone so quickly that I was not sure.

During the latter days, just before the bulldozers

moved in I made some observations on butterflies. Towards the fence by Bolton's Farm I saw a peacock butterfly settled on a patch of primroses. Over a period of time I saw the tortoiseshell and red admiral. The orange tip and the painted lady made a brief appearance, but a number of the meadow brown mixed and fluttered with the common white for a longer period than all others.

Once I found the spoor of a fox, but he kept himself well hidden and came out at night. I saw him once in the headlights of a car. An old dog fox, his eyes glittered as he looked over in my direction, and then he was gone, across Commercial Road, down into the ditch and vanishing into the bushes and long grass towards Gresham Road. I searched for him for many months without success. When the Council yard had been built he was still causing concern. I have recently learnt that one of his successors is seen now and again in the Council yard area. Perhaps he is the sole survivor of the wealth of wild life which I have described.

Architectural Walkabout

Old Buildings

Kingston Road
Victorian Cottages (George Street)
The Malt House
built between: 1824 & 1851

Fairfield Avenue
Victorian Houses

High Street
Late Georgian & Victorian buildings visible above shop fronts (Nos 28, 30 & 56)

Thames Street

Hook On & Shoot Off Cottages	c1800
Iron Railway Bridge	1856

Market Square

The Blue Anchor	
upper front	1700
ground floor front	1904, 1915
South Wall rebuilt	1982
Town Hall	1880
Shops	17th/19th Cs

Clarence Street

Literary & Scientific Inst	1835
(corner of Bridge Street)	
Clarence House No 31	c1833
Staines Bridge	1832

Church Street

(E end) Nos 21-26	Cromwellian
Nos 45-53	early Victorian
Bosun's Hatch No 103	18th C
GW Rly station house (west end)	c1820
57 Church Street	
earliest part	1737
additions before	1815
Malthouse rear of No 57	post 1737
The Brewery — the tower	1903
The rest	1872 and 20th C
The Beeches No 111, 113	1803

with additions now 2 separate houses	1836, 1852
Corner Hall	1600 & later
Various houses	18th & 19th C
The Lammas/Ashby Recreation Ground (approach from Binbury Row)	
The London Stone	1285
Existing pedestal	1781

Vicarage Road

St Mary's Church	1828
tower	1631
Duncroft	1600
extensive alterations	18/19th C
Moor House	1867

Modern Buildings

London Road

Telephone Exchange	1973/4

Kingston Road

Congregational Church	1956
United Glass	1964
Spelthorne Civic Centre	1972

Fairfield Avenue

Housing Development (The Moormede Estate)	1970s

High Street

Elmsleigh Centre	1979/82
Debenham's	1955/66
Johnson & Clark	1956 and 1981/2

Laleham Road

Block of flats	1960s

Market Square

Flats, west rear of Town Hall	1980

Church Street

Cambria Court	1930s
Housing Estate, Church Island Close	1979/80

Notes to the text

1 See Kevin Crouch; *London & Middlesex Archaeological Trans* vol 27, 1976.
2 See *Victoria County History (VCH) Middlesex vol II.* Information in this section was supplied by E. A. Pearse.
3 Information about Thomas Lord Knyvett was supplied by R. Miles.
4 The author is indebted to research by J. Livermore for the information in this section.
5 See Edward J. Burrow, *Borough Guide for Staines & Egham* No 237, Cheltenham 1912.
6 Information about swan upping was provided by the late Richard Turk, sometime Royal Swanmaster in the Staines Local History Journal (SLHSJ) 2 pp27-33 of December 1967.
7 Close Rolls, Henry III, 1236 & 1261: grants of timber for repair of the bridge. The first Act relating to the bridge (1 Henry VIII cap 9) provided for persons to take tolls, to repair the bridge and to account for expenditure.
8 It has been maintained by some writers that a second iron bridge was built to replace Paine's bridge, but there seems no evidence to support this.
9 The bridge was released from tolls in 1871 with much local jubilation, the last cart across was a decorated donkey cart and the toll gate was thrown in the river with cries from the crowd of 'down with old England' (the name of the toll keeper). Research by J. Orr.
10 Witnessed by the late C. R. Smithers.
11 This information comes from a lecture by the late W. F. J. Hamblin.
12 See David Parry's *English Horsedrawn Vehicles.*
13 Staines had two annual fairs, on 11 May for horses and cattle, and on 19 September the onion fair which included toys, corn, apples, parsnips, spices, salt, cattle & pigs. The fairs continued into the 20th century. Now there are just two weekly market days on Wendesdays and Saturdays in the Market Square, but they bear no relation to the old fairs whose tradition went back to 1228.
14 PO Directory 1878. VCH describes him as 'coachbuilder of note'.
15 From the *Borough guide to Staines & Egham* No 327, 1912.
16 This and much other information for this section was provided by E. A. Pearse in SLHSJ I, June 1967 pp3-12 and 2 December 1967 pp40-50.
17 From a thesis on Staines bridge by J. Orr.
18 Information from the late Jack Taylor in SLHSJ I, pp17-19.
19 This information came from the late C. R. Smithers.
20 In Swinburne Lane there were once a few cottages where forestry workers lived. They made charcoal in the vast aspen forest, which stretched between Staines and Hounslow, for use in the gunpowder mills at Hounslow and Hanworth.
21 'Fire Brigade under Local Board: Captain, first officer, second officer and engineer, and nine gentlemen and four working-men', from *Dictionary of the Thames;* Charles Dickens, Jr, 1891.
22 Information from the late R. Crimble JP.
23 Information from Mrs Elsie Cleary. The steam fire engine 1830 and the first motor fire engine 1904 appeared respectively on the 8p and $3\frac{1}{2}$p British commemorative stamps issued in 1974 for the 200th anniversary of the Fire Prevention (Metropolis) Act.

Bibliography

Ashby, Robert; *Some Records of the Ashbys & Friends of Staines, 1757-1916*; Privately lithographed 1916.

Bawtree, Maurice; *The London Coal Duties & their Boundary Marks*; *The Rickmansworth Historian* No 8, Autumn 1964.

Bolland, R. R.; *Victorians on the Thames*; Midas Books, Tunbridge Wells 1974.

Brayley & Brewer; *A topographical & historical description of London & Middlesex*; Vol V 1816.

Crouch, Kevin; *The archaeology of Staines & the excavation at Elmsleigh House*; Spelthorne Archaeological Field Group publication.

Dictionary of National Biography Vol XI, Oxford Univ Press, 1937/8.

Holt, J. C.; *Magna Carta*; Cambridge Univ Press, 1965.

Ingram, Arthur; *Horsedrawn vehicles since 1760*; Frederick Warne (Publishers) Ltd, Blandford 1978.

Maxwell, Gordon S.; *Highwayman's Heath*; Thomasons Ltd, 1949.

Pevsner, Nikolaus; *Middlesex*; Bernard Leon, 1951.

Post Office Directories

Railway Magazine, Vol 101 No 648, April 1955; Tothill Press Ltd.

Rolt, L. T. C.; *The Inland Waterways of England*; Geo Allen & Unwin, 1950.

Surrey County Council Town & Country Planning Committee; *The Administrative County of Surrey*; County Council Pubn, 1976.

Thacker, F. S.; *The Thames Highway*; David & Charles, Newton Abbot, 1968.

Vale, Edmund; *The Mail Coach Men*; Cassell, 1960.

Victoria County History for Middlesex Vol II; Oxford Univ Press.

Below: Swans with cygnets.   *N. Smithers*

Below: Ladies Thames Punting Championship, 1938.
Author in foreground!